The P

MW01076240

THE PURSUIT OF GODLINESS

Five Centuries on Spiritual Ascent

Bishop Irenei
of London and Western Europe

HOLY TRINITY PUBLICATIONS
The Printshop of St Job of Pochaev
Holy Trinity Monastery
Jordanville, New York
2025

Printed with the blessing of His Grace,
Bishop Luke of Syracuse
and Abbot of Holy Trinity Monastery

The Pursuit of Godliness: Five Centuries on Spiritual Ascent
© 2025 Matthew Craig Steenberg

An imprint of:

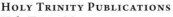

holytrinitypublications.com

ISBN: 978-0-88465-499-5 (paperback)
ISBN: 978-0-88465-514-5 (ePub)
Library of Congress Control Number 2024945758

Cover art: Mosaic, "The Winged Stairway to Heaven," Kykkos
Monastery, Troodos Mountains, Cyprus.
Source: Scan of Meisterdruke print by Holy Trinity Publications.

New Testament Scripture passages taken from the New King
James Version. Copyright © 1982 by Thomas Nelson, Inc. Used by
permission.— Psalms taken from *A Psalter for Prayer,* trans. David
James (Jordanville, NY: Holy Trinity Publications, 2011). — Old
Testament and Apocryphal passages taken from the *Orthodox Study
Bible.* Copyright © 2008 by Thomas Nelson, Inc. Used by permission.

Printed in the United States of America
Versa Press Inc. 1465 Spring Bay Road, East Peoria, IL, 61611
versapress.com

Contents

Introduction

It has seemed to me useful to consolidate together some of the most essential teachings of the Holy Fathers on the attaining of a Godly life, since we find ourselves sojourning in a world increasingly bereft of, or rather, antithetical to, the pursuit of Godliness. It is true to say that the modern Christian finds himself surrounded by a rising sea of error and hostility toward truth and faith, and truer still to say that this generation is sorrowfully weakened in its resolve to stand against their opposites. Yet we are the sons and daughters of the crucified and risen Lord, and the whole of our Christian tradition—that which has been faithfully handed down to us through pious generations, from the Apostles to our own day—compels us to believe that the pursuit of Godliness is not only a necessary and possible work in this world, but that it is essential to the fulfillment of our humanity.

God made it possible for us to attain to communion in His life the moment He fashioned us of His will and design, with His own hands, vivifying us with His breath. This is the very purpose of our existence. Apart from its pursuit we are perpetually dehumanized; but through it, the human creature has it within its nature to attain "to a perfect man, to a measure of the stature of

1

the fullness of Christ" (Eph 4:13). The fullness of Christ—the life of the incarnate God! If modern man has lost sight of this high calling and impetus for his sojourn, he must be reminded by the Church, in her saints, of what is true and essential, so that he may be saved from the darkness he seems inexplicably to prefer.

The Church stands ready to provide this guidance, now as in every age. Indeed, her unfailing mission across the millennia, even since the foundation of the world, has been precisely this: to expose man to that which changes man; to speak the words of life that lead to a transformation of life. Saints and teachers, martyrs and ascetics, have labored precisely to this end: to convey the mystery of the Life in Christ, which has the unique power to draw each human creature into a life greater than his own—to live a life that can be united to God's.

The teachings that convey this are nothing apart from the Church that delivers them to us, in which they live and breathe and retain the potency of the divine Grace by which they have been authored. I stress this at the outset, because we live in a generation in which teachings and life are too often separated; in which Christian thought is divorced, wittingly or unwittingly, from lived existence within the Church. But if a person is ready to submit his or her life to the Church—which is Christ's Body, which He heads, which is the Grace-bearing fount of all the Fathers' wisdom—then the teachings they have inscribed on the hearts of her faithful can touch even our own, and give us the means to be raised to a newness of life.

So this small project of dwelling upon their teachings, and conveying as best as I am able a glimmer of their timeless witness, specifically as it pertains to the pursuit of Godliness in this broken world. In setting forth these essential testimonies,

I have found it here, as elsewhere,[1] useful to adopt the format of "centuries," or collections of one-hundred short expositions, in order to make more readily accessible the thoughts of our Fathers and the traditions of our Church that are spread across hundreds of volumes spanning two millennia. I call to mind the words of the divine St Maximus, who wrote in the preamble to his adoption of this same format, "I have gone through the writings of the Holy Fathers and collected from them passages relevant to my subject, condensing much material into short chapters and in this way making it easy to remember and assimilate."[2] If such consolidation and condensing were useful in his day, when Christians were more adept than in our own, how much more might such a format be useful in our generation, when short paragraphs, which can be read one at a time and contemplated as is beneficial, might speak to hearts unaccustomed to the lengthy treatises of our more robust ancestors.

I beg the reader to read what follows with patience, paying attention to what is useful (which we pray reflects that which comes from the saints, which comes from God), and overlooking the inelegance of my language or the cumbersomeness of my presentation. May God bless that, despite my inadequacies, a shimmer of the light of divine knowledge that has shone forth from our spiritual ancestors may be found in these pages; for what we learn from the saints we try faithfully to convey—this is the essence of our inheritance as Christians. Saving words are not invented, but received. May we only be faithful to the teachings the Lord's Church has preserved for our salvation!

+ BISHOP IRENEI
April 2024

I

A Century on the Kingdom of God and Its Attainment

1. Created in love by the Father's Wisdom, molded by His two Hands and placed upon the earth as the adornment of creation, the human creature, God's own handiwork, is called to no less than the attainment of divine Life. The Kingdom of Heaven is his charge and the object of his spiritual journey; for in the Kingdom the commingling of the human and divine reach their zenith and stretch to all eternity, and in this, man, at last, finds his true and abiding home.

2. The purpose of our life is therefore singular, as our creation was singular: to attain the fullness of the Lord's embrace in beholding the everlasting light of His Kingdom. Man has been created to inherit the Kingdom of his Maker.

3. The human creature is created for glory! Let no demonic lie or worldly despair rob you of this profound hope. In your heart is the Lord's vision of creation, and within you all creation is united. The same heart that you hold in filthy hands, debasing it with every passion and whim, is a heart that can contain the living

God—a heart that can become a diamond in which all the beauty of the cosmos is visible.

4. No Father has put this more eloquently than the illumined St Makarios, who said: "The heart itself is only a small vessel, yet dragons are there, and lions; there are poisonous beasts and all the treasures of evil; there are rough and uneven roads; there are precipices; but there, too, are God and the angels; life is there, and the Kingdom; there, too, is light, and there the Apostles, and heavenly cities, and treasures of grace. All things lie within that little space."[3] Think of this, Christian! Think of what mystery it is that abides within you! Think of it, and be neither prideful nor afraid; for God forged you as so great a wonder, capable of discovering greater wonders.

5. It is in this same heart that man tastes, in this created life, the glory of eternity. When the Lord proclaims "the Kingdom of God is within you" (Luke 17:21), He speaks not of some interior object that man contains as a kind of possession; He speaks, rather, of this sacred mystery—that in man's heart the Kingdom of eternity is made accessible to the creature in time.

6. Precisely in this most sacred space (if it is made a temple of glory rather than a bereft and barren dwelling) the Lord manifests the Kingdom toward which man is ever called. The spiritual man is therefore able to discern within himself the heavenly habitation for which he has been created, revealed by the Lord in his heart. He does not, cannot, do this alone; no power of intellect, however piously motivated, leads a man out of self-will and to a right perception of what lies within him. But if he permits his eyes to be opened by the Grace of God in His Church, and if he

submits to being led rather than demands to do the leading of his life, he finds the Guide of his heart dwelling within his heart, revealing there a foretaste of the garden of Paradise.

7. The man who is spiritually aware yearns for this divine habitation, wholly conscious that his heart will not rest until it rests in the Lord,[4] and that in this life he has "no abiding city" (cf. Heb 13:14). He feels himself a sojourner in every place, still at his beginnings as he reaches every milestone, always craving that greater calling he has already tasted and touched, which ever propels him forward along the ascent of holiness.

8. He who is blinded to the truth, yet not wholly insensitive to his own nature, does not fully perceive this divine orientation of his creation and calling, yet senses still that he lives for a higher purpose. His spiritual senses may not function well, but they function still. He, however, who is both blind and insensitive, denies his nature and calling, and even acts against them; yet they remain the true impulses of his heart, even amidst his denial.

9. We must therefore strive to regain the perception of our true nature, and of the gifts of God that impel us toward His Kingdom, lest we spend our whole lives battling against what is real within ourselves—accepting "the sin which so easily ensnares us" (Heb 12:1) rather than the reality of the divine image that truly defines us. Reality is not mutable, truth is not "mine" and "yours"; there is truth and there is error, wisdom and delusion. We must choose which we wish to embrace, and live accordingly.

10. We begin our small labor here, referring to this reality at the outset of our words, for we discover in it one of the most sorrowful

spiritual illnesses of our latter age: man has lost the spiritual vision to see God. He has blinded his eyes and is too insensate to recognize even that he can no longer see; yet in his audacity claims greater sight and vision than all who have gone before him.

11. This blindness may have external contributing factors, but it is chiefly the result of an interior disposition. One who does not wish to see, will not—and that wish is expressed not in a deliberate choice (few indeed determine outright that they wish to be blind), but rather in modes of life and thought that, willingly embraced, bring about such a result. This is revealed to us already from the ancient desert: "There is no point, while we are still blind, in asking why it is we cannot see the light; no point in stuffing our ears and then asking why it is we cannot hear anything."[5]

12. The man who is blind in spiritual sight cannot rightly see at all, for even what he beholds with his physical eyes he fails correctly to perceive—and what he cannot perceive, he cannot understand. When the world as a whole succumbs to this spiritual blindness, is it any wonder that it stumbles from suffering to suffering, wounding itself ever more grievously both by what it does not see and by what it wrongly perceives?

13. We can rightly call this blindness madness, for when a man sees not with spiritual eyes, he perceives sensory reality instead through the lens of his fantasies; and the fantasies provoke passions that bind this man's "sight" to the proclivities—and, too often, the perversions—of his heart. His sight is more projection than reality.

14. Thus he arrives at the point where he can stare at the sun and claim it is not the sun, or a rock and claim it is not a rock, fulfilling in himself the prophecy of Jeremiah, that he and his suffering

kin have become "foolish and heartless. They have eyes that see not" (Jer 5:21). How the prophets of old speak anew to our present generation!

15. This madness, let us well understand, is a result of the loss of the spiritual orientation of man's heart. There can be no eyes to see in one whose heart does not pulse with spiritual life. Yet he who attains to spiritual things suffers no blindness, even if his physical eyes are wholly without power (and we have witnessed this in numerous great saints of our age); and he who acknowledges the reality of the spiritual, even if lacking a perfect contemplation of it, is preserved from the dark void of spiritless non-sight.

16. However, a man who denies the spiritual will stare into his brother's face and see not a man, and into God's, and see not the divine. How perilous, that we have come to such days!

17. Do you see how the abandonment of a spiritual orientation dehumanizes the human creature? Man was made to see, yet makes himself blind. He was made to understand, yet renders himself a fool. So the beautiful creature that God fashioned from the dust begins to fade away to become obscured, and creation groans that it sees ever less clearly that icon of God's beauty that was crafted to be its crowning glory.

18. The man who disregards his high calling indeed loses sight of himself, and the man who does not know himself is, of all creatures, most wretched—for even the animals are true to the nature God has fashioned in them and abide by the calling of His Will. In this, if we may say it, even some of the irrational creatures have a spiritual lesson to teach God's rational flock. In all of creation, only man has gone astray with regard to its perception of God.[6]

19. How long, then, shall our race debase itself below the most brute of beasts? Or even, we might say, beneath the insensate and inanimate elements of creation; for as the Lord declares, even the rocks and stones know how to fulfill their purpose and sing to the glory of their Maker (cf. Luke 19:40). This creature, then, this wonder of dust and bone that the Maker of all things has fashioned into a being worthy of His own breath, yet which discovers (or rather, creates) in itself such darkness and filth, must learn from those stones, and from all other creatures, the nobility that resides in everything God has fashioned, and strive to reclaim what he has lost.

20. God fashions only the beautiful; His nature is capable of producing no other. Further, He calls that same creation toward His beauty, and to nothing else; for the Lord Who creates in love fashions that which is capable of love in return—and through this, to be drawn into His own life.

21. The Kingdom of God is therefore the natural culmination and fulfillment of man's creation, not some manner of external "addition." There, and there alone, does he find the perfection of that in which he was created from the first. There he finds himself, made whole: the glorified creature of earth, breathing with God's own breath. He does not lose himself in eternity; rather, he finds what had been lost, and by which he is at last made complete.

22. The love we taste now is but a foretaste of that love; the peace we experience now is but a glimmer of that eternal peace. These gifts draw us toward the Giver of gifts, that we might in the fullness of time have fulfilled what we now experience in part.

23. How glorious, therefore, and how wonderful, is the promise made to man! Of all the incomparable richness and beauty of this life, he has beheld within it only the glimmer of a light infinitely brighter, yet set before him.

24. The cure for the underlying disease of our modern age resides in restoring its perception of such spiritual things, and its awareness of the Kingdom beyond this world. To live without these is not fully to live, but to cling only to the faintest tendrils of life; not to stand with eyes open, but with the faintest rays of light passing through closed eyelids—and yet still believing that one sees.

25. Worldly madness is often the result of a surfeit: an excess of fantasy, an uncontrolled imagination, a surplus of disorganized and impassioned thoughts. Spiritual madness, by contrast, stems not from a surfeit, but a want: a want of active spiritual perception in the heart and mind of man. This is what ultimately renders him spiritually mad.

26. When this world again acknowledges the world beyond, when the creature once again acknowledges its Creator, it will be saved from its madness. This reclamation of sanity must start in the heart; but it can spread from the heart to encompass the whole world.

27. The Christian in society should strive to aid the fallen world in this necessary remedy for its suffering, ever calling the culture around it to live of and for its Creator to the degree that he or she is able. However, while not every man has authority over states, powers, or cultures, every man is able to have authority

over the kingdom of his own heart, and there is no excuse not to exercise this authority rightly.

28. The Christian who does not take possession of the kingdom of his heart, willingly hands it over to the demons; and he who gives up his soul, who chooses darkness when the Light is offered, makes pathetic a heart that could be an eternal temple for the glory of God.

29. If you will be strong, then, you must stand fast in the contest and make up for what is wanting in your heart through careful observation and obedience. It is time not to lament or to long, but to work; for the Kingdom, as the Lord says Himself, belongs to those who "take it by force" (Matt 11:12).

30. In undertaking this labor, we must diligently observe what is good and what is poor within us, and then obediently receive the correction required to increase the former and eradicate the latter. This is the continual task of the spiritually watchful life. It requires steadfastness and humility, as well as instruction and guidance.

31. If, through such watchfulness, a man finds that he is suffering from the spiritual madness we have described, let him understand that his spiritual vision is weak and that the remedy for his condition begins in re-orientating his awareness toward the reality of the Kingdom of God. For surely, as our Fathers teach, "wherever a person's heart is given, wherever their deepest desire draws them, this is indeed their god. If a disciple's heart longs always for God, then God will surely be the Lord of the heart."[7] If, therefore, it is observed that the heart has given itself to some other "god," let it be our utmost task to re-direct its longing, to give it to what is better, that it may turn from falsehood to Truth.

32. Give the heart what the heart deserves, the glory for which it was created, and it will do what it was created to do: course spiritual life through the veins of the fleshly creature and lead it to the deepest realities of its genuine nature.

33. He who perceives the Kingdom of God while yet in this life understands the true nature not only of himself, but also of this world, for perception of the divine informs sensible perceptions: the revelation of the Creator, which opens the heart, enables the creature to perceive the purpose and form of creation around him.

34. The awareness of the Kingdom of God is thus a sun shining genuine light upon the created realm, for by these rays we behold the world in its intelligible beauty, as the purposeful handiwork of the Artist of creation.

35. It is this perception that grants sight to the eyes and wisdom to the mind. An intellect can only reliably discern good from evil when this wisdom resides within it. Without the awareness of the Kingdom of God, good may seem to man as an evil, and evil a good.

36. For this reason the demon pushed our first mother to abandon the word and awareness of God; for in his cunning deceit he knew that, thus turning from such awareness, she could be persuaded that what the Lord had clearly informed her was evil, was in fact a good to be sought and obtained (cf. Gen 3:1–6). It was not the distinction between good and evil that he secretly longed to bestow upon her, but the disintegration of that very distinction.

37. Likewise our first father, Adam, discovered the darkness of madness when he, following his wife, closed his eyes to the reality

God had fashioned and chose to interpret creation without Him. So blind and foolish did he become that he felt he could flee and hide from God, running from the One Who was racing after him, seeking to provide him with the blessed opportunity for repentance (cf. Gen 3:8, 9).

38. How much suffering could Adam have avoided, had he only, in that moment, reorientated his eyes toward God and His Kingdom, rather than away from them! With his eyes turned away, he saw God as a pursuer and punisher (cf. Gen 3:10). Had he turned to face the Lord in humility, he would have found Him with arms mercifully outstretched, seeking naught but Adam's departure from sin and restoration to His love.

39. Thus would humility have been Adam's immediate route to the restoration of divine knowledge and Grace. For, as St John pondered, as "the angel Lucifer fell from heaven solely on account of one passion, his pride, it makes me wonder whether it might not be possible to rise up to heaven solely on the strength of humility."[8] Through the deceptive promises of pride Adam came to know nothing at all; through humility he might have come to know all things.

40. Without humility, man looks to himself rather than to his God, and discovers despair where he could as easily find redemption. It is thus that the demons suffer; their pride is a constant source of sorrow, unyielding and fierce. Shall man follow them forever? Or shall he eventually learn that in humility the door to redemption is opened, and the way out of suffering illumined?

41. So it is with every man who looks to the earth instead of heaven, or who looks to the earth in ignorance of its heavenly

origin. He will invariably discover fear and suffering where there ought to be peace.

42. This earth has its origin in heaven, or rather, in the God of heaven. He fashioned it as a foretaste of the eternal Kingdom, as a nursery to raise up His children to the fullness of life. When its Maker is denied, or this sacred purpose ignored, the earth becomes a shadow of itself.

43. In the shadows of ignorance lurk demons and despair. Beware, therefore, of making dark what the Lord has created in light.

44. The Holy Fathers speak of "earth" in both positive and negative senses. Positive, because it is the handiwork of God Who only creates the good, and in its truest nature is a work of artistry that points ever toward its Artist; but negative, also, because in the hands of man, rebelling against the Maker of all, the earth is disfigured, rent from its true nature, groaning under the weight of humanity's sin (cf. Rom 8:22).

45. When the Fathers speak negatively of the earth, they speak of the idol the earth has become through man's blindness and folly. The Lord Himself, however, shows that it is an idol only by man's influence; by nature, it remains ever capable of the good for which it was made and ever the possessor of its primal beauty. And the Lord, moreover, is always prepared to reclaim it for that noble purpose.

46. Thus the eternal, only-begotten Son, perfectly manifesting His Father's will, came not apart from creation, but through it and in it. When "the Word became flesh and dwelt among us … full of grace and truth," we "beheld His glory" (John 1:14), not only

in the earthly advent of His eternal Person, but in his taking up of dust, of Adam, and showing its sanctified and glorious nature.

47. In Christ the eternal Kingdom and the kingdom of this world are united, the assumed creation healed through its union with the Divine.

48. Christ, the fulfillment of Adam and the "last Adam" (cf. 1 Cor 15:45, 47), thus reveals the perfection of the human creature, which is the pinnacle of the created realm. We behold our very nature, material and earthly, bound indissolubly to the Divine in His Person.

49. In this, the same Christ shows us the true nature of that material creation, for dust and bone became His in the incarnation. Matter, though distinct from God in origin (for God has no origin, and all matter is His handiwork), nevertheless may be united to what is Uncreated, itself becoming eternal.

50. We see in our Saviour Jesus Christ the revelation of the Kingdom of God as it pertains to this world; or rather, we behold in Him that which the Kingdom of God reveals about this world. It is fallen, but can be raised up. It is temporal, but can be made eternal. It is corruptible, but can be united to incorruptibility and shine with the uncreated splendor of God Himself.

51. This is the reason we, reciting the Beatitudes in the Divine Liturgy, intersperse the words: "In Thy Kingdom remember us, O Lord."[9] We seek not the Kingdom as if it were a distant place into which Christ goes, but as the reality in which He always exists and which He reveals to us, calling us toward it and toward Himself.

52. The Holy Fathers have shaped our liturgical prayer explicitly to remind us that only in the awareness of this Kingdom can we understand the words of Christ: "Blessed are the poor in spirit…", "Blessed are those who mourn…", "Blessed are the meek…" (Matt 5:1–11) and the rest. Apart from the awareness of Christ Who comes "in His kingdom" (Matt 16:28), even the Beatitudes are reduced to little more than encouraging sentiments. With that awareness, however, they are revelations of the true nature of existence in this life.

53. In worldly terms, the meek inherit nothing: they are dispossessed and become fodder beneath the feet of temporal rulers and powers. But when a man sees this life with the perception of the Kingdom, he can say with Christ that these meek are blessed, and that precisely in their meekness they shall inherit the earth (cf. Matt 5:5); for the power of men comes ultimately to naught, while the humble are united to the nature of the self-humbling God Who reigns forever.

54. In worldly terms, one who opposes us is our enemy, and our enemy is to be feared, and fought, and fled from. But in the awareness of the Kingdom of God, we discover that our enemies are our benefactors, for they provide the possibility of humility and exercise in the virtues. They are gifts, if we will let them show us a higher path.

55. In worldly terms, death is the opposite of life and a thing to be at all costs avoided and put off, for it is seen as the cessation of existence itself. But in the awareness of the Kingdom of God, a man discovers that death has been destroyed (cf. 1 Cor 15:26), and that though its presence remains in this

world until its consummation, it no longer stands as "the end" or the cessation of life. Life has conquered death, and life reigns (cf. Rom 5:17).

56. Do you see how the awareness of the Kingdom of God alters, or rather grants, man's perception of reality? Through this awareness alone, whole worlds are altered. In each of these examples, the object of man's reflection is the same: meekness, or an enemy, or death. But how different is that which is perceived! Apart from the Kingdom they are dark; in the light of it, they are beautiful and fill us with the hope of eternity.

57. This is why the Apostle Paul says, with regard to death and those in repose, "I do not want you to be ignorant…lest you sorrow as others who have no hope" (1 Thess 4:13). Without hope in the true reality of God's Kingdom, death is the triumph of evil and the ultimate reference point of all suffering. But for those who persevere in the hope of the Kingdom, such sorrow is only momentary, knowing that "the dead in Christ will rise" and we shall, with them, be ever with the Lord (cf. 1 Thess 4:16, 17).

58. The world around us is wont to consider all such reflections, when it acknowledges them at all, as if they pertain solely to religious arenas: religious talk restricted to the realm of religious things. It does not understand that this same reality affects all human perception and experience. In our day, as we behold man's turning from God and abhorrence of His Kingdom at an ever-expanding societal level, what do we discover? That the Church with her "religious ideas" falters? Far from it: while false religions fall, the one Church grows only stronger in times of trial. No, rather we see every element of social and civic life affected and faltering, while the Word of the Lord remains steadfast.

59. Man abandons an orientation toward the Kingdom of God, and he ceases to call good, good, or evil, evil. Rather, he comes to speak in positive terms of "self-definition," "subjective morality," and "personal truth"—the very things that, if he retained his spiritual perspective, he would consider most sinister and dangerous.

60. In this abandonment man ceases to acknowledge the realities of age, sex, race, or any of the other distinctions by which God has ordained the beauty of the interwoven handiwork of creation. Instead, while speaking tirelessly (or, we might say, tiresomely) about "diversity," he in fact destroys diversity; for while the forms of society's madness outwardly seem multitudinous beyond counting, at their core they are but different manifestations of a singular reality: the false belief that the only thing that is genuinely real is my self, and everything else is but a construct.

61. Of all generations, to be pitied most is that which cuts the throat of the true diversity of creation—the fact that the Lord made each according it its kind, multiform and distinct, each with unique natures and callings, and beholding the great symphony of this diverse creation saw that "it was very good" (Gen 1:31)— and instead replaces it with the selfishness of man's singular lust for self-definition.

62. Do we not readily behold the fruits of such non-spiritual selfishness in our own day? Man focuses wholly on himself, he strives to be free by his own self-definition of freedom, he gropes after "happiness" as an idea defined entirely within himself, he seeks to cast off as shackles anything taught, or received or inherited from generations of wisdom and truth—and what is the end result of all this intellectual brazenness? His heart laments. He seeks

happiness, but discovers sorrow. He craves freedom, and finds himself a slave. He desires wisdom that surpasses all ages before, but no longer even knows his left from his right.

63. His confusion thus leads to a moral and ethical captivity. When a man enslaves himself to sin, when society binds itself to delusion, then the very concept of "society" falters; for the individual man no longer helps himself, and in the society of men one no longer aids the other, but rather brings the other to their mutual harm. Such a "society" ceases to call a male a male, a female a female, a family a family, truth truth, and so on, instead redefining such terms to conform to its lusts and selfish desires—despite the obvious harm this causes to all. The whole race seeks the path of Cain rather than that of Abel (cf. Gen 4:1–16), brother destroying brother and bringing the race to shame.

64. Civil societies thus cease to be truly civil entities, and become mere collectives of men in common rebellion, their individual inhabitants shells of the fullness of human existence. Look around you, and behold these truths made real on all sides! Man, having lost the vision of the Kingdom within himself, becomes ever more limited in his vision. Where he could behold eternity, he beholds finitude. Where he could see divine things, he becomes barely capable of discerning what is before his very face.

65. Do not succumb to this! It is a spiritual disease, yes, and one most grievous; yet the point of identifying it as such is to prepare the way for healing, for spiritual diseases can be cured. It is the substance of man's self-made grief; but ours is a Lord Who wipes away tears from the eyes of the grieving (cf. Rev 21:4).

66. If you have succumbed in some degree to this illness, acknowledge that it is precisely that: an illness to be laid before the Physician of souls and bodies—and do not despair. Recognize, even if for the moment you receive it as a promise rather than a reality you wholly experience, that there is more beauty in you than you have yet seen; that there is more glory to be held in your grasp than you have yet known; that in God's Hands, there is more to life than what you have yet tasted.

67. I never tire of re-reading the story of Abba Joseph of Panephysis, whose revelation to a fellow desert-dweller disclosed this reality to all generations most beautifully: Abba Lot went to see Abba Joseph and said to him, "Abba, as far as I can I say my little office, I fast a little, I pray and meditate, I live in peace as far as I can, I purify my thoughts. What else can I do?" Then the old man stood up and stretched his hands toward heaven. His fingers became like ten lamps of fire and he said to him, "If you will, you can become all flame."[10]

68. Let this witness ever be with you. Without the vision of the Kingdom of God shining in our hearts, we see but flesh and blood; but with that vision alive within us, we see flesh and blood shining with the flames of uncreated glory, united to the Uncreated God Who lifts us up to Himself.

69. The entrance into this union with God's glory comes through a life of sanctification shaped by repentance. When an awareness of the Kingdom of God fills the mind, the heart is led to shed those affectations that keep it from this Kingdom, and turn away from them toward the gates of Paradise.

70. This repentance is an active change of the heart; a change of life. Mere sorrow or regret does not alter the path of life: one must gain the resolve to walk anew, along a different path, toward a different goal.

71. The gates of repentance open to those who stand before them unadorned, unassuming, and craving nothing other than the mercy of their Lord. To these, repentance becomes a pathway that leads inward to the holy depths of a purified heart. But to those who stand at these gates and demand entry through pride or entitlement, the bars hold fast.

72. Once a man has set foot upon the path of repentance, his heart falters with every backward glance he takes. The faltering ascetic is too often like Lot's wife, who looked back during her divine rescue and became a pillar of salt (cf. Gen 19:26). So it is with every clinging focus upon the past. Do not be hardened through your memory of your old life, but advance with every step toward the repentance that leads to Life eternal.

73. Repentance is an abandonment: an abandonment of the world and the passions, to be wholly embraced by the love of God. It must represent a break with the life that has gone before. One cannot cling to the wrongs of the past while striving for the glory of what lies ahead.

74. Repentance is a labor, and one that requires the whole heart, soul, and body. Say to your soul, when it grows sluggish in this quest: "You trifle about in idleness, and then lament that no real repentance lives in you. Alas, 'my mind stops, my tongue is silent, and my hand grows numb for you—I wonder and am astonished at how you are unable to exert yourself even a little!' But rise up,

work, and do not look back, and you will behold the gates of Paradise grow closer day by day."

75. But while it is a labor and work, the path of repentance is nevertheless sweet, for it is the entrance into the garden of the heart, where there bloom flowers whose color is only for the Lord and which bring indescribable delight to the soul. Few see this garden or taste of its sweetness, for the entrance—true repentance—seems unbearable to many. If only a man could sense aright the joy that lies beyond the heavy, iron gates of this garden, he, and the whole world, would rush toward it.

76. The soul is weakest and most dissolute when into this garden are invited those seeming friends who reside outside its walls. When the garden of the heart is no longer reserved for the Lord, when it is instead made into a place of abode for all and sundry, its flowers wilt and its radiance diminishes. And then, even should a man find himself within it, he does not taste that sweetness or joy that he knows it once possessed.

77. By these seeming friends, we mean the passions and attachments to which we have grown accustomed through a lack of diligent watchfulness. Chief amongst these is self-love, which is "mindless love for the body"[11] and by that false-love becomes the "mother of evils."[12]

78. How can we tend to the garden of the heart, whose beauty is directed toward God, when the true object of our love is not God but our own lives? We deceive ourselves through the love of ourselves.

79. The close friend of this self-love is sensual pleasure, which focuses our senses and interior faculties on the momentary

satisfaction of their untrained urges. Here we behold the antithesis of the created faculty of the heart, which turns in on itself and seeks to receive, rather than to give, in defiance of the admonition of the Lord (cf. Acts 20:35).

80. These two seeming friends (we say this because, though they are in reality our fiercest enemies, we treat them as friends by giving them a familiar home within us) produce avarice, as our Fathers tell us[13]; and avarice "is a root of all kinds of evil" (1 Tim 6:10). Thus this trio of false friends, when permitted access to the inner recesses of the heart, stirs up within humankind all the sins of rebellion. "It is because of them that wrath, anger, war, murder and other evils have such power over mankind."[14]

81. But amongst these seeming friends, who are too frequently granted access to the inner places of man's heart, we must also list those of his kin, be they linked to him by blood or the bonds of earthly friendship, who seek not his purification and salvation, but rather the furthering of passionate desires and rebellion against Truth. While true spiritual friendships are amongst the greatest blessings bestowed in this life, and while the bonds of blood may likewise be most blessed, as we see in the enduring love of Christ for His mother, the antitheses of these—anti-spiritual relationships and ties of kinship that lead away from God rather than toward Him—can of all things in this life be the most destructive.

82. A genuine longing for the Kingdom of God, and an active striving toward it, does not preclude friendships in this life; but it must define them, shape them, and grant them their character.

83. A true friend joins hands with him who walks toward the Kingdom, supporting his steps and aiding in the prevention of his falls. Such a one is a fellow companion of Paradise, already in this world; a signal and strength of the life that lies beyond.

84. But beware the one who comes in the guise of a friend yet does the opposite. He is no true friend who takes our hand and leads us to destruction, or who precipitates our fall rather than strives to prevent it.

85. If a test of true friendship or of the spiritual health of familial relations is required, let it consist of such questions as these: Does the time spent in the presence of the other lead us toward a more Godly life, or away from it? Do the lingering impressions of the times spent together bring an increased desire for a zealous keeping of the teachings of the Church, or a longing instead for laxity? Is the fruit of our interpersonal communion a craving for ascetic fortitude and spiritual growth, or self-gratification and stagnancy? Such questions are not hard to answer, if only we will keep watch over our hearts; but they require resolve to accept, and to become the causes of action.

86. The Creator Himself said, "It is not good for man to be alone" (Gen 2:18), but we must understand that temporary solitude is better than collaboration in evil, or the rendering lukewarm of a fiery faith. Therefore, seek pious companionship of the kind the Lord blesses, and flee its opposite.

87. The awareness of the reality of the Kingdom of God causes a man to guard the purity of his heart, and moreover, to long so to do; for therein he tastes that Kingdom's presence. It causes him

to reject foreign invaders into this sacred space and repent of all interior impurity, for by such repentance the heart comes to life and the blindness of his spiritual eyes is cast away.

88. Repentance and spiritual sight are, therefore, close kinsmen. As Abba John teaches, "If we purify ourselves of wickedness, then we will come to see invisible realities."[15] Such sight is healed not by optometrists or the curing of the diseases of the flesh, but by the witness of the saints and the curing of the disease of sin.

89. It is by this restoration of spiritual vision that the Christian will not only begin to realize the full reality of his created nature, drawing ever closer to the Holy Trinity through the Grace that unites him to divine Life, but he will also begin to fulfill his mission in the world; for what the soul is in a body, this Christians are in the world[16]—and the illumined soul is thus the illumination of creation around it.

90. The Christian's mission to the world consists fundamentally in the transformation of his own heart. In that space are worked wonders that touch every corner of the cosmos.

91. It is therefore in the power of every Christian to change the whole of creation and to touch the life of every other human being. None are isolated; none are far from the possibility of pastoral care and the exercise of redemptive compassion. Repent, attain the Spirit of Peace, and, as St Seraphim once said, "thousands around you will be saved"—and even beyond these, countless more whose lives are changed when the human race is healed in your heart.

92. As the world around us ever more dramatically loses sight of the Kingdom of God, the Christian for his part must the more fiercely reclaim it. The more the world turns from God, the more

completely the Christian must surrender to Him. The more the world mocks God, the more the Christian must love Him. As the world rebels against the Lord and His Will, so the Christian must wholly submit himself to God in free obedience and hope. In this way, he joins the Lord in saving the world.

93. This, I think, is what that our holy Father St Justin meant when he said, "The ascetics are Orthodoxy's only missionaries. Asceticism is Orthodoxy's only missionary college. Orthodoxy is ascesis and life, so its mission is preached and accomplished only through ascesis and life."[17] May he who wishes to bind up the wounds of our world, hear these words and understand them.

94. In our day, man lives his life almost exclusively externally: it is a world of social activism, social media, social morality. But a man who does not act within his heart, does not truly act at all. Ascesis is the only true means of changing the world at its core.

95. The integrity of man's interior life shall therefore always be the mouth by which he speaks most potently to society. The words that emanate from an unpurified soul shall never have the power to save others, however beautiful they may otherwise be. But the words of the Godly are lights that lead the stumbling to sure salvation.

96. Whence come such light-filled worlds and the examples of life that lead to the Kingdom? From the Kingdom of God itself, and man's experience of it! The Saints speak with divine authority because they have tasted of divine things; they have the power to lead us toward the Kingdom of God because they have touched it, and it has given them strength. They are men and women truly alive, because their lives have been shaped by God's.

97. We call them saints because we recognize that they have attained holiness. They embody the goal set before us all. Their lives are, and must be, the guideposts of our own.

98. Following their example, may the love of the Kingdom of God enflame our hearts also. May it reclaim for man his life, and for society its soul. Modern man must look beyond, to discover what lies within; and purifying what is within him, he may yet become a "lamp on a stand" that brightens the universe (cf. Matt 5:15).

99. "Wherever you go, keep God in mind"[18]: thus did our Father Anthony exhort his disciples unto salvation. This counsel is timeless, and modern man is parched with thirst for such clear words. Let us only heed them, lest instead of the water of life (cf. Rev 22:1) we fill our mouths with sand, and mindlessly wonder why our thirst is never quenched.

100. If we will but do this, God will surely lead us into His Kingdom with open arms. Only let us be as humble as we must be obedient, following the words of St Theodoros: "Knowing these things, let us fear God and keep His commandments, so that we may be perfect and entire in the virtues. And having a humbled spirit and a contrite heart, let us repeat over and over again the prayer that the great saint Arsenius used to offer to the Lord: 'My God, do not abandon me, though I have done nothing good in Thy sight, but because Thou art compassionate, grant me the power to make a start.'[19] For the whole of our salvation lies in the mercy, and in the deep love, that God has for us. To Him be glory, dominion, and worship forever. Amen!"[20]

II

A Century on Love

1. The Kingdom of God, as the abode of Love, will not be obtained by those devoid of love, for a house divided against itself cannot stand (cf. Matt 12:25). Therefore, Christian, strive to obtain love in this life, that you may participate in its fullness in the next.

2. The Apostle Paul exhorted: "Now abide faith, hope, love, these three; but the greatest of these is love" (1 Cor 13:13). The Christian must stand himself upon the firm rock of these chief virtues, knowing which is the crown and perfection of the others.

3. How can love be greater than faith, as the Apostle says? Because authentic love is faith's truest offspring, her pinnacle and perfect fulfillment. Without her child faith is but a barren mother, just as without her parent, love is but an energy of self-will. When, however, love is born of faith, then faith itself is proved vivifying, granting, and fulfilling our hope.

4. As "every tree is known by its own fruit" (Luke 6:44), so the authenticity of faith is proved by the love to which it gives birth. If it is divine love, a love that is greater than the knowledge of all

mysteries or than prophecy, or than even the tongues of angels (cf. 1 Cor 13:1–2), then we know that it is the fruit of authentic faith, and the faith that has produced it is to be cherished and preserved.

5. If, however, the so-called love a man finds in himself is that fashioned in his own image, driven by emotion but devoid of divine power, then he knows by this sour fruit not only that his love is insufficient, but also that he has yet to attain a true faith in the God Who "is love" (cf. 1 John 4:8) and bestows genuine love upon those who believe in Him; for withered fruit proves the barren nature of its tree.

6. Love is the authentic test and confirmation of faith. "Faith by itself, if it does not have works, is dead," says the Lord's brother (Jas 2:17), but faith without love is not even the carcass of real faith, but merely a manufacture of human design.

7. Here is a sure test of the love that is in you, provided by the Apostle: Does it suffer willingly? Is it free of all envy and pride? Does it resist provocation? Does it refrain perfectly from every evil thought and intention? Does it rejoice in truth and flee wholly from iniquity? Does it abide in moments when all worldly powers fail—when tongues, knowledge, and even prophecy fail (cf. 1 Cor 13:4–10)? If so, then what is in you is divine love, which God has stirred in your heart. But do not be proud!

8. If, however, the love in you seeks its own (i.e., the attainment of the comforts of the body or the swell of emotion), or if it claims to seek the good in another but secretly rejoices in his falls, or if it speaks flowery words about righteousness and virtue but inwardly rejoices in iniquity, then this is not love that

comes from God but from the shifting sands of the world—and woe to him who builds his house upon the sand, for when the wind, rain, and floods shall come, great shall be the fall of it (cf. Matt 7:24–27).

9. He who lives his life in the exercise of such worldly "love" experiences a foretaste of hell. For what is the chief characteristic of hell, if not the embrace of what is fallen in place of what is divine? Or, the clinging to that which leads the heart into suffering, rather than into redemption?

10. But, just as hell is a distinct reality from heaven, separate unto eternity and not, as some in our day wrongly teach, the singular reality of heaven "experienced differently," so we must understand the distinction of natures in this life, also. Love which fails the test of the Apostle is not love wrongly experienced or defined or embraced: it is quite simply not true love at all. It is a thing to be expunged from the heart as a poison that, while perhaps not immediately bitter to taste, leads surely to perdition.

11. When we discover such false "love" within ourselves, woe to us if we feel satisfied with the idea that this love, while not perfect, is nevertheless a stepping stone to righteousness. False love is not partial holiness: it is the fruit of the demons and the antithesis to the divine life within us. We must seek after what is true, not the shadows of truth that abide in falsehood.

12. It is easier for a man wholly insensate to love at all to plant it within himself through faith and the exercise of the virtues, than it is for a man filled with false love to release himself from his delusions and seek after what is right. False love is a passion that takes swift possession of the *nous*, compelling it in the supposed name

of righteousness down a path that leads only away from the King-dom of God.

13. You, therefore, who wish to take your spiritual life seri-ously, must constantly watch over that which rises in your heart in the name of love. The most powerful virtues are opposed by the most powerful vices; and it is the lot of the wicked, as St Thalassios says, to take the vices for virtues.[21] Watch, therefore, and question the love that is in you, to see if it be true or false, righteous or evil, and act according to the teachings of the Fathers in either case.

14. Especially when we are too much intermingled with the world, we find, upon the examination of our hearts, that we have permitted false love to be born within us. This happens when the heart is influenced by worldly conceptions of love, and mirrors in itself what the senses behold around it.

15. For this reason, seek solitude within the reasonable possibil-ities of your circumstances. True love of God and brother is born not of the images received from excessive companionship, but of the divine imprint found when a heart withdraws from worldly preoccupations and inwardly calls upon the Name of the Lord.

16. Of this we have again the divine Thalassios as our teacher: "The person who is unaffected by the things of this world loves stillness; and he who loves no human thing loves all men."[22] And in the ancient desert the same lesson was taught, as Abba Arsenius said to Abba Mark, "God knows I love you, but I cannot be with God and with men. The countless hosts of angels have only a sin-gle will, while men have many wills. So I cannot love God and be with men."[23]

17. St Arsenius is of course speaking to monastics and those who abide in monastic renunciation are saved from such external provocation, but only if they take their renunciation seriously. A monastic community can be the fortress that holds at bay the world and its crafty fingers. These fingers seek ever to impress themselves upon the soul and reshape its clay into a new and debased formation. But one who abides in such a community voids himself of this protection if, having entered into such a fortress, he allows the enemy in through the gates by remaining attached to worldly discourse and concerns.

18. How many in our day fall into this trap, since the conveniences and technologies of modernity so easily insert themselves even into environments of isolation and contexts of renunciation. But one can never truly claim to have left the world if he brings the world willingly with him as he goes; and the solitude of the monastery can never wholly transform the heart of one who will not accept the rejection of worldly attachments.

19. However, let none think that the monastic enclosure itself is sufficient to break the bonds of worldly influence and generate divine love in a monk's heart. The monastery and the monastic's vows of renunciation are tools blessed by God's Church to accomplish spiritual ends; but the actual accomplishment of those ends depends not only upon the tools, but also upon how we wield them. He who enters the monastic life but retains his worldly orientation is like a man given a hammer but who immediately sets it aside, and later wonders why the nail is never driven into the wood.

20. The same thing may be said also of life in the world. Monastics hold no monopoly upon salvation or its attainment,

and God grants abundantly to those who live in the cities, in families, and in civil society the tools necessary to overcome the passions. Our merciful Lord leaves none bereft! But there, too, the tools of spiritual combat must be not only offered, but received, taken up and wielded.

21. He who believes he lacks the tools required to gain love, deceives himself and mocks God's mercy; but he who believes the tools alone will save him, mocks both God and himself.

22. The tools the Lord provides us to obtain divine love are threefold: firstly, the exterior practice of practical love of neighbor; secondly, the interior discipline of love of God through the exercise of the virtues; and thirdly, the obtaining of divine communion through ascetical discipline. These can, and must, be practiced by monk and layman alike, and have the same power to transform both.

23. By the first method, a man fights the impulses of self-will and worldly compulsion by emulating in his relationships the love of God toward His creatures. By the second, he quells within himself the passions that draw the heart away from divine love, reorienting his inner life toward what is higher and nobler. By the third, the man thus freed from worldly compulsion and oriented toward the sacred, receives in his soul that which is purely divine, participating in true Love through his communion in God's very life.

24. Let us understand, therefore, that there is a path to love that is laid open before each human being, and the means to walk along it toward that goal. God gives to each, and to all, both the means and the methods to arrive at His Life.

25. The first method is that to which the Lord so often exhorted His Apostles and disciples during His coming upon the earth, incarnate in the flesh. "You shall love your neighbor as yourself," He said, and called this the second great commandment, inextricably bound to the first: "You shall love the Lord thy God with all your heart, with all your soul, with all your mind, and with all your strength" (Mark 12:30–31). By this, the Saviour bound love to what we have already described as its birth-giver: faith. The faith one has toward God is only whole and real if it gives birth to genuine love—both of Him, and of our neighbor.

26. God does not ask you to love anyone: He commands that you love all. A commandment is not a request but a law, and one that leads to Life.

27. This commandment of love of neighbor is not issued solely or even chiefly as respects sentiment, but action. In speaking the parable of the man who fell among thieves, the Lord showed that he was neighbor to that fallen brother "who showed mercy upon him;" and He exhorted His followers, "Go and do likewise" (cf. Luke 10:29–37). Love of neighbor, like love of God, must not exist merely in thought but also in deed.

28. That man, the traveler from Samaria who bound up the suffering man's wounds and cared for him, showing him such mercy, did not know the one for whom he cared. He did not place upon his love a test of friendship, kinship, or worthiness. Rather, he loved because such was the nature of his heart, not on account of the demonstrated merit of the other.

29. He who loves as God loves, must likewise love without respect of person or position. As St Maximus says, "Blessed is he

who can love all men equally"[24]; and in another place, "He who gives alms in imitation of God does not discriminate between the wicked and the virtuous, the just and the unjust, when providing for men's bodily needs," since "God, Who is by nature good and dispassionate, loves all men equally as His handiwork."[25]

30. If you love only those who love you, what good is that self-serving love (cf. Luke 6:32)? Indeed, how can you claim to have any love at all, when what you enact is only a transaction, bestowing in recompense for what you have received, or hope to receive? The money lenders in the Temple court did the same, and the Lord drove them out for their evil ways (cf. John 2:13–17).

31. A man who does not strive to love all equally, loves no one truly.

32. A man who loves no one truly, cannot love God or be born of God's love. Therefore, love your neighbor, and all your neighbors, for by this key the door into the Kingdom of God is opened.

33. Make your beginning by recognizing that the obligation of love is one a man owes to every creature, whether they have of their will become evil or sought the good.

34. There is none born evil, and thus none born unworthy of love. It is only our preoccupation with social merit that causes us to see one as worthy and another unworthy; but a man is not merely the sum of his actions, and his value does not reside in his choices—right or wrong—but in the fact that he is, by his very formation, the immediate handiwork of the Lord.

35. Genuine love toward one's neighbor seeks his good in all things: where he possesses virtue, that it might be strengthened and perfected and bestowed upon the world; where he demonstrates wickedness, that it might be corrected and his wounds healed, so that in due course virtue might replace it.

36. As a foundation for all else, of course, he who is hungry must be fed and he who is naked, clothed. Remember, in your moments of self-centered debasement, that feeding the hungry is a greater work than raising the dead, as our divine teacher, St John the Golden-mouthed of Constantinople,[26] once taught.[27] Call this to mind the next time the temptation rises to ignore the material needs of a brother or sister: this thought will surely set the God-fearing man in his place!

37. If you have not helped your brother in his need, you have proved yourself wholly devoid of love. Moreover, the Lord will disregard all your other ascetical or "spiritual" labors, as He Himself declares; for on the last day "He will also say to those on the left hand, 'Depart from Me, you cursed, into the everlasting fire … for I was hungry and you gave Me no food; I was thirsty and you gave Me no drink … inasmuch as you did not do it to one of the least of these, you did not do it to Me'" (Matt 25:41–46).

38. Genuine love therefore has a beginning in the giving of alms to the needy. Physical alms are necessary; and a yet higher good to be joined to these are spiritual alms—for even a starving man does not live "by bread alone, but by every word that proceeds from the mouth of God" (Matt 4:4).

39. The clothing of the naked, likewise, does not consist solely in the provision of physical clothes (though the Christian should always race to provide for the physical needs of those in want), but also in the spiritual garments of piety and divine Grace. We show love to the needy not only when we assist them in meeting their earthly needs, but also in raising them beyond earthly want by instilling in them a communion in the "one thing needful" which, once embraced, will never be taken away from them (cf. Luke 10:42).

40. Love toward neighbor, be it Godly love, always leads beyond the present moment, into eternity; it propels the recipient of love beyond his temporary circumstances, into the stability of eternity with the Lord.

41. Such love must therefore, with respect to those with whom we are close enough to act fraternally, consist not in sentimental adornments or the acquiescence to fallen desires, but in the agreeable correction of faults and the mutual admonition of the ways that lead to life.

42. He who feigns to love a brother, but does not seek to lift him out of the self-inflicted suffering of his passions is like a doctor who pretends to care for a patient while refraining from providing him with the medicine to cure his ailment. Love does not confirm a brother in his wrongs, but seeks to set him on a new and better path.

43. Likewise, love that seeks to provide only emotional comfort at the cost of the correction of deadly error is not love but a deceptively concealed curse. He who knows his brother is harming himself through his mode of life, and does not rise with

appropriate action (whether interior or exterior) to stir that brother to compunction and change hangs a millstone around his neck while pretending it is a garland of jewels.

44. In urging that we "not grow weary while doing good" (Gal 6:9), the Apostle teaches that love must be tireless and relentless: it must not grow weary when it is not returned, nor falter when it does not bear immediate fruit, recognizing that there is always an interval of time that elapses between sowing and reaping.[28] Remember the extent of God's love for us: for in spite of centuries of care and correction through the prophets and patriarchs, the Law and countless divine visitations, as our sin nevertheless abounded and increased, God "so loved the world that He gave His only begotten Son" (John 3:16). Shall you, then, claim to be His child, and not be prepared to sacrifice yourself to the offering of love toward your brother?

45. God's mercy toward us in our wretched sin did not consist in comforting us in our transgression, but in providing the means of repentance by which we might depart from it. Bear this in mind always in the love you show your brother. Help him out of his sin; do not sin against him by confirming him in his own.

46. This is the hardest when the love a man shows earns him not gratitude but rebuke; but here the sacrifice of love is the most necessary. The guards at the Lord's crucifixion did not thank Him for His sacrifice, but mocked and taunted Him; yet Christ did not abandon His sacrifice of love for them, "for they did not know what they were doing" (cf. Luke 23:34). In that moment, they of all men were most in need of the very love He was perfecting before them.

47. The man who hates you, you must accept and receive as a divine gift; for we can see even in ourselves that the advent of such emotion is in general a consequence of internal suffering, and thus evidence of the need for the grace required to heal it. If this is true within us, so too in our brothers and sisters! Thus, in "being kind to the unthankful and the evil" (cf. Luke 6:35), we are provided with the opportunity to find great reward in emulation of the Most High God who dispassionately loves all alike, both those who do good to us and those who do not.

48. A man who is spiritually healthy does not hate, nor act in evil ways. Therefore, recognize in the hatred witnessed in others, especially in the hatred directed toward you, something not to be condemned but understood as a fruit of such struggle, and thereby find compassion. In this way you will save yourself from judgment.

49. It is the devil who wishes you to condemn the man who works evil against you—for then he wins your soul as well as your brother's. But God commands that we love our enemies (cf. Matt 5:44; Luke 6:27), as we might hope for such love to be directed toward us by those we wrong. It is precisely when we are the most spiritually ill that we are most in need of care and correction.

50. Accept, therefore, every evil and slander cast against you in response to the love you show. More than this, rejoice in it. Hold in your heart the words of our Saviour: "Blessed are you when they revile and persecute you, and say all kinds of evil against you falsely for My sake. Rejoice and be exceedingly glad, for great is your reward in heaven, for so they persecuted the prophets who were before you" (Matt 5:11–12).

51. Rejoice, the Lord says, in such circumstances. Rejoice! Indeed, the man who learns to rejoice in the evils done unto him in response to love, has learned to embrace his Saviour's heart, for he thus acquires a growing affection for those who abuse him.[29] Surely, he will see divine things.

52. If, however, you are weakened by your passions and unable immediately to rejoice in such circumstances, at least guard yourself from bitterness or anger. These are poisons that prevent joy from ever arising. Forbid them access to your heart, and it will in due course learn to rejoice in the emulation of its Redeemer.

53. To prevent bitterness or anger, bridle your tongue. The tongue, provoked to respond in kind to evils spoken against it, not only permits the poison of anger into the heart, but even tills the ground so that the poison will be absorbed the more swiftly.

54. Respond to anger with silence, and you will be blessed a hundredfold.

55. No matter what provokes it, St John Cassian reminds us, anger blinds the soul's eyes, preventing it from seeing the Sun of righteousness.[30] Not only will you surely not see your brother's heart or true need if anger blinds your sight, but you will also not see God, since, as St John also says, "anger, whether reasonable or unreasonable, obstructs our spiritual vision."[31]

56. When at times a direct response to another is required (let the Spirit be your guide: for there are times when piety demands that words must be spoken), remember always that a word is a powerful sword. Wielded well, it can cut the evil out of your brother and free him unto eternal life. Wielded passionately, it can kill him. We each will answer to God for our words, and for our silences!

57. The great ascetic St Mark taught us that rebukes may be given in malice or self-defense, or out of fear of God and respect for truth.[32] Learn the meaning of his words and you will be protected from evil-doing; the distinction is the difference between the salvific edge of a surgeon's blade, and the mortifying thrust of an assassin's knife.

58. Remember also his counsel that it is better to pray devoutly for your neighbor than to rebuke him every time he sins.[33] Love corrects intermittently through words and actions as may be necessary, but ceaselessly through prayer on behalf of our brother who struggles alongside us.

59. If in these ways a man exercises himself diligently in the practical love of his neighbor, he emulates the love of God toward His creatures. But if this is only infrequent, or sporadic, it will not defeat a man's self-will (for it is no great accomplishment to exercise love only when we feel so inclined). If, however, it becomes a spiritual discipline to practice such love always, in every circumstance, then the impulses of self-will are subjected to the divine command and worldly compulsions are gradually shifted.

60. A Christian must never choose whom to love, for he must love all; nor may he choose when to love, for the time is never "tomorrow" or "later," but always "now;" nor yet may he choose how to love, for he must love as God loves, even if it cost him everything—unto his own blood.

61. Remember the holy counsel of St Isaac, who reminded his hearers that the Son of God was not bound to death as a "required" means of forgiving sins, as if His granting of

forgiveness were dependent upon some prescribed act; rather His death on the Cross was the ultimate, the perfect, demonstration of His love.[34] Christian love requires a Cross: do not think that you will escape yours. Rather, "take up your cross, and follow Me," says the Lord (cf. Luke 9:23), and this cross will lead you to heavenly places.

62. Live thus, and love thus, and your love will be the fruit of a truly Orthodox faith; it will crush the passions of pride, self-will and self-gratification, which are the roots of so many other sins. It shall equip you, also, to take up the second tool that prepares the soul for divine love: the exercise of the virtues, which builds an interior disposition disciplined in the love of God.

63. By such exercise, a man quells the passions within himself, and through this obtains a freedom unknown to one who is enslaved by self-will. Only a free man truly loves; though we speak here not of the supposed "freedom" of this world, but the freedom that comes from fulfilling the commandments of God, and thus being confirmed in His likeness.

64. Earthly slaves are denied the full expression of love through their physical and cultural bondage: thus the great sin of this denigration of man. But he who is the slave of sin, even if it be sin "freely" chosen, is likewise denied the fullness of love—for his supposed freedom has in fact bound him all the more completely to the narrowness of his transgression.

65. The Law of God commands the departure from sin and the exercise of virtue, since the former draws the heart away from divine love, while the latter reorients man's inner life toward what is eternal and impassible.

66. The very categories of sin and virtue describe not arbitrary preferences on the part of God, as if He deemed one act this and another that without reason; rather, they are evidence of His compassion toward His creatures. The Lord seeks to preserve in peace and blessedness all that He has fashioned, and save it from sorrow; and the Creator knows better than the creature what leads to each.

67. Every vice draws us further from God, while every virtue propels us closer to Him. Therefore one who seeks divine love must become practiced in all the virtues, drawing by each step closer to the God of love. He must abide no hindrance in this spiritual labor, and disregard no aid.

68. The transformation of our interior disposition is precisely that which leads to a transformation of the heart; the commandments are therefore the corrective tools of a loving soul. Thus do we hear from the great lamp of Optina: "A monk must unfailingly be a doer of all the Lord's commandments, an emulator of the state and order of the bodiless ones, a knower of God and of all love towards Him and his neighbour."[35]

69. Do you understand this Holy Father's words? They are not only for monastics. He speaks to his fellow monks as to lights for the whole world:[36] only by becoming virtuous through fervently doing what the Lord commands, do we come to know the angelic love of God and man. One cannot pretend to be the Lord's disciple and not follow His commandments.

70. St Theophan counsels likewise: "The possibility and basis for all inner victories is first the victory over ourselves: the breaking of our will and dedicating ourselves to God, with the inimical denial of everything sinful."[37]

71. So we begin more clearly to see that the victory over ourselves comes not from a force within ourselves (i.e., from our own design or rationale of approach), but from the Law of God that reshapes our broken vessel into a fitting receptacle for the Grace of the Holy Trinity. Every commandment, therefore, must be understood as a means to recraft the broken heart unto love; and the Christian must embrace every tool, and wield it well, in order to attain this life.

72. Again we hear the familiar words: "Man shall not live by bread alone, but by every word that proceeds from the mouth of God" (Matt 4:4). Learn from this rebuke of the devil by our Saviour that every divine commandment is to us as a saving nourishment, without the eating of which we wither.

73. Be eager, therefore, to be fed by this heavenly food. Do not contrast in your mind the keeping of the commandments with the practical works of love. The commandments make a man capable of love by creating the space for love within him. Do you think you will be able to give what you have not yet received or attained?

74. The attainment of this divine love through ascetic discipline, then, is the third tool. The Lord wishes you to love as He loves, with His love, as the embodiment of His image. He thus leads you along the ascetical path in order that this image may be brought to perfection in you.

75. It is only in a man fully alive by communion in the Spirit that the glory of God's creation is wholly manifest; for this man truly alive in Christ, and no other, is he who bears both the image and likeness of his Creator.[38]

76. The ascetical disciplines of the Church are the means by which we take this present life, this amalgam of soul and body that is our very being, and, having disciplined it through the keeping of the divine commandments, make it ready to be united to the fullness of Grace that sanctifies the work of God's hands.

77. Through our ascetical endeavors, the stone of the heart is made soft flesh (cf. Ezek 11:19, 36:26); or, to take another image from our Fathers, the dry soil of our hearts is moistened, becoming clay that can bear the imprints of God's hands.[39] Such is the true fruit of asceticism: not the hardening of man into a cold religious militant devoid of love, but his softening through fierce means into that which can be shaped by Love Himself into what love desires.

78. Such ascetical discipline takes what we have rendered insensate and restores to it the ability to think and to feel. It takes the beast that man has made of himself, and gradually renders him human once again.

79. It is here, when through long, ascetical exposure to the waters of repentance the clay of our soul has once again become tractable, that we can be shaped by a force other than ourselves, into that which is better than the hardened "self" we had become. And this is what the creature most sorely needs: to live not unto himself, but unto God.

80. Thus what is in us might become no longer solely the manufacture of our will or designs, however pious, but the life of the soul vivified directly by its communion in the Holy Spirit, to Whose presence we become more and more acclimated through the ascetical softening of the heart.

81. The Spirit binds man to Christ, Whose life the Christian has "put on" through sacred baptism (cf. Gal 3:27),[40] so that in due course he might be able to say with St Paul, "I have been crucified with Christ; it is no longer I who live, but Christ lives in me" (Gal 2:20). Of all the Apostle's beautiful utterances, perhaps none is more spiritually profound than this; for St Paul discloses the mystery at the heart of human existence: that we, in our unworthiness, might be so drawn into the life of Christ that His life becomes ours, even as ours have always belonged to Him—that the world might come to see in each Christian life the presence and Grace of the Creator of that life, Who is the Creator of All. This, be assured, is the high calling of communion set before every Christian soul.

82. We seek this sacred communion as the highest good of creation. In it, a man tastes of the fullness of love, and the love that he in turn bestows upon the world is no longer his own alone, but God's.

83. This the Holy Fathers call the deification of the creature, or *theosis*, for we begin to live in God and God in us, united by Grace to the Giver of Grace.

84. This deification is at the same time an "anthropification,"[41] for only the deified man is truly human, according to the desire of the Creator. Only he has moved beyond the limitations of nature into true personhood through his communion in the Trinity of Persons that is our God. But these mysteries are perhaps too great for the feebleness of our words.

85. We must not, however, use the weakness of our perception as an excuse not to struggle upward along the path to sanctification

in Christ. All are called to ascetical discipline, since all are capable of transformation.

86. Fasting withers our reliance on the flesh and gradually sets us free from the tyranny of the appetites. Through this small ascesis, man is encouraged toward freedom—and thus he grows a step closer to Love.

87. Discipline in prayer, likewise, serves the ascetical end of limiting our self-will, which was the cause of the rebellious angels' revolt against the love of God.

88. Obedience to the Church, and to those rightly appointed by her to look after us, is also a tool of ascetical transformation. Through obedience we cut off selfish understandings and break through the limitations of the fallen intellect. Through it, we are returned to the state of our first ancestors before their rebellion and made capable of the growth that had been their lot.

89. The scrupulous attendance at Divine Services, especially long vigils, is yet another ascetical tool by which the appetites and habituations of the flesh are curbed and Godly longing restored to the soul.

90. Moreover, in the Divine Services our ascetic struggle—that which we bring forth from our labors, with God's help—is met with communion in the Divine Mysteries that the offices provide; that is, the mystical Grace that is brought forth to us. This is the miracle of our worship. In every Divine Service of the Church, man reaches toward heaven and heaven bows toward the earth.

91. The world will find it hard to see how a vigil, or a fast, or adherence to the spiritual word of our priest, might correlate to

an increase in love; but the Christian understands, with spiritual comprehension, that by these means the selfish man, the "old man" with his evil ways (cf. Col 3:9), is transformed into the "new man," renewed in the image he bears, which is the image of God. It is thus, and only thus, that he becomes capable of true love.

92. Your ascetical discipline will save you, not by evoking some merit or worth or accomplishment in your individuality, but by drawing you close and uniting you to Christ, your Saviour.

93. Your ascetical discipline will not teach you love; that is the role of the divine commandments, and it is for this reason that the Lord provides them and that the Christian must heed them. It will, rather, unite you to Love and make you a vessel of true love in the world.

94. Do you see, therefore, how the ascent of love is one and the same with the ascent of salvation? In seeking love, we are not seeking some pious benefaction—we are seeking God. In striving to acquire love we are not striving to lay hold of a mere quality or characteristic of life—we are striving to lay hold of salvation itself. In loving our brother, we are not hoping to become his benefactor or inspiration—we are hoping to lift him up into the love of Almighty God, by which act we are ourselves raised up in that love, that together as His children we may attain eternity in His image.

95. When, thus, a man acquires true Love, he acquires Life. He becomes a *person*—that is, one whose identity is bound up inextricably in his communion with the Trinity of Persons, which is, in itself, the nature of authentic personhood. He becomes

fully human, for this divine communion has always been that for which human nature was fashioned by God.[42]

96. The pursuit of love is therefore the essence of the Christian life. We receive love, and we learn to offer love back to Him Who "first loved us" (1 John 4:19).

97. We can therefore confidently say that he who does not love is not a Christian, whatever the other aspects of Christianity to which he might lay claim. When we fail to love, we deny our baptism; but when we exercise love at a cost, pouring it out with our blood, we experience the washing of baptism anew. So by laxity toward this virtue man can lose his soul, but by its attainment he can be perpetually renewed in the Grace of eternal life.

98. All the Scriptures, all the Sacraments, exist as the fruit and the manifestation of Love. Let none be so foolish as to think the experience of their power can be gained without it.

99. Therefore, Christian, learn what is truly needful! Abide in faith, hope and love, as the Apostle exhorts—but let your faith be real and your hope divine, for then they will give birth to their greatest companion: the love that transcends this world and "abideth forever" (cf. 1 Cor 13:13).

100. Glory to God, Who gives the gift of love, the gift of His own being, to the works of His hands: the Father, the Son and the Holy Spirit. Amen!

III

A Century on the Acquisition of Knowledge

1. Spiritual knowledge is the ripe fruit of love. Wisdom follows from a purified and sanctified heart, while an unloving man will never possess understanding.

2. This we have heard from the illumined teacher of knowledge: "All spiritual contemplation should be governed by faith, hope and love, but most of all by love. The first two teach us to be detached from visible delights, but love unites the soul with the excellence of God."[43] Love is the governing principle of real knowledge; by being united to Love, man draws closer at one and the same time to the Truth.

3. It is fruitless to seek after spiritual wisdom, therefore, without striving to acquire love as its foundation. It is for this reason that we reflected on love first, that we might not be tempted to approach knowledge without it; for such "wisdom" thus advanced, will always bear the imprints of its worldly origin and remain attached to its birth-giver.

4. How many, especially in our day, suffer in soul and mind—and bring untold suffering to others—through the attempt to gain

spiritual knowledge without becoming detached from worldly intellectualism. They try to mingle oil and water, the result being neither one nor the other: neither water that quenches thirst, nor oil that brings "joy to the heart" (cf. Prov 27:9).

5. True spiritual wisdom is an illumination of the soul by the Holy Spirit, a communion in Truth through Him Who is Truth (cf. John 14:6), and a mercy of adoption by the Father of creation. Its origin is in the self-revelation of God to man, not man's attempt to discern the nature of God.

6. Without the illumination from above, human attempts at divine wisdom merely recycle the transgressions of the tree in Eden (cf. Gen 3) and the tower in Senaar (cf. Gen 11:1–9). Man seeks to grab hold of what he has not yet been given, and by contrivance to claim heights he has not rightly attained.

7. St John Chrysostom puts this clearly when he speaks of men ruled by the soul without the soul's illumination from above: "He is soulish (*psychikos*) who attributes everything to the rea-sonings of the mind without considering that he needs help from above, which is pure folly. For God bestowed the mind so that it might learn and receive help from Him, not that it should consider itself to be sufficient unto itself. Eyes are beautiful and useful, but if they strive to see without light, their beauty profits them nothing, nor their natural form, and the act may harm them. So also with the soul: if she strives to see without the Spirit, she becomes an impediment to herself."[44]

8. It is the same reality that St Diadochus has in mind when he says, "It is right always to wait, with a faith energized by love, for the illumination that will enable us to speak. For nothing is so

destitute as a mind philosophizing about God when it is without Him."[45] Man must learn, therefore, the types of knowledge that are accessible to him, as well as the means of their obtainment; and he must always remember that silence is a wisdom unto itself, and one accessible to all.

9. If we take the words of the Fathers as our trusted guides, we find that these illumined saints reveal the measures of knowledge, both the sturdy and the so-called, showing us the means of attaining what is trustworthy and pure, and avoiding what is but a trap of fallen man. They call "philosophizing" the act of vainly seeking a higher knowledge through lower means, or attempting to attain divine wisdom through analysis devoid of spiritual contemplation.

10. Knowledge of exterior things is gained by observation and the deliberation of sensory images. This is a natural knowledge, in that it is grasped through the observation of nature; but it is incomplete, even in its most exalted forms, since it perceives nature in a sensory way and appreciates it through a deliberative capacity.

11. Nevertheless, such natural knowledge can disclose much. Man has been given the book of the world as his source for this knowledge, for "the entire body of creation stands in the place of books and writings about God," as the great preacher said.[46] This is the first sourcebook for the soul, for "never at any time did she see of herself, but she had creation as a book, laid openly before her."[47]

12. The soul thus has at her disposal the richest treasury of wisdom in the form of creation, which the Lord Himself

fashioned to guide her into knowledge and worship. "The sky is beautiful," writes the Golden-Mouthed, "but the purpose of its formation was that you might adore its Maker; the sun is brilliant, but it is there that you might worship its Creator."[48] In this reality we behold at once the unfathomable love of God toward us, Who elects to fashion the whole cosmos for our benefit and edification; and also the hard-heartedness and stony intellectualism of man, who has for ages beheld this open book of the created realm and yet so often not elected to gain from it the knowledge of Truth.

13. This is because, when it is approached solely externally, knowledge is intrinsically finite—even when focused upon the works of the Infinite One. Such exterior knowledge can only ever go so far.

14. Knowledge of interior things, however, adds to this the intellectual assessment of that which is intangible, yet perceptible through the other faculties of the intellect. This is a higher knowledge, for already it steps beyond the physical limits of creation and perceives what physical senses alone cannot disclose. Then there is a higher knowledge still: knowledge of spiritual things. This, however, is gained solely by communion in the Spirit, and is the highest form of wisdom, for it is the direct illumination of the creature by the Creator, Whose perfect knowledge sets aflame the heart and mind of man.

15. Human faculties may make a soul ready for this communion, but can never manufacture it; just as a sower may make ready the ground for the seed, but cannot manufacture the seed itself. Such comes only from God (cf. 1 Cor 9:10).

16. The tilling of the soil of the soul, which readies the ground for the illumination of divine knowledge, takes many forms, of which the Holy Fathers disclose to us several: "Spiritual knowledge," we hear, "comes through prayer, profound stillness and complete detachment, while wisdom comes through humble meditation on Holy Scripture and, above all, through grace given by God."[49] By this counsel we are again taught to distinguish between "wisdom," which is a Spirit-led perception of external and internal realities, and "spiritual knowledge" which is communion in the Spirit Himself.

17. Spiritual knowledge is both beyond all exterior and interior wisdom, and at the same time the perfection of these. A man possessing spiritual knowledge understands the more perfectly all created natures, even as he is given to gaze into the mystery of the Uncreated.

18. Knowledge of the natures (which the Greek Fathers call the *logoi*) of things can be attained to a high degree through natural means, as we have said; but it is the one who knows the Maker of natures, the Logos Himself, that perceives them the most clearly.

19. The ascent of spiritual knowledge is therefore eternal, for by it man comes to participate in the Wisdom of God Who is boundless and infinite. There is no limit, no end, to the human ascent into divine knowledge, but man is ever "transformed … from glory to glory" (2 Cor 3:18), and, as St Gregory says, becomes one "never ceasing growth in good, never circumscribing perfection by any limitation."[50] Or, as St Irenaeus says most succinctly, "God shall forever teach, and man shall forever learn."[51]

20. It is for this reason that St John can declare that "far better than the heavens is man, and it is possible for him to possess a soul brighter than their beauty"[52]; for the heavens are beautiful and bright in the fixture that God has established for them, and demonstrate their radiance in remaining ever as the Lord has fashioned them—but man has the ability to grow beyond the bounds of his first formation, to ascend in holiness and truth and to grow ever closer to his Maker.

21. Only the human creature can grow and learn in this way. Other creatures may learn and adapt through their experience of the physical world in which they dwell (let us not pretend that beasts cannot learn of their surroundings, or tender animals grow in their understanding of their environment); but only man can prepare his intellect to transcend the world and ascend eternally toward higher things.

22. Yet as much as the ascent is eternal, since God is eternal, so much is man hindered at its first steps by his clinging to the opposite of love, which, as we have said, alone gives birth to wisdom and leads to knowledge. This hindrance is fuelled by man's confusion over life and death, fear and love, which stills even the most nobly intentioned heart in its ascent to spiritual knowledge and divine Life.

23. Modern man believes that the opposite of life is death, and thus strives in all things to avoid the latter so as to retain the former. But a wise mind knows that death is not the opposite of life; true life lies not in the prevention of death, but in the conquering of it.

24. The opposite of life is fear, for fear leads man away from God, into the realm of the captivity of death and the clouding of the

intellect. It is fear that sticks man fast in the mud of sin; fear that causes him to cling to his own will, rather than God's; fear that turns him from repentance; fear that darkens his mind and blinds him to spiritual and even material reality. In short, fear turns man from Life, and that which is not life is death.

25. If then the opposite of life is fear, not death, then likewise the opposite of death is not life. The opposite of death is love, for love leads man beyond his passions and into the embrace of the Saviour, Who defeats death anew in him and lifts him up to divine things.

26. Therefore, he who wishes to see divine things, to be illumined by spiritual knowledge, must cast out fear. By so doing, he embraces Life which produces love and conquers death, uniting him to God Who "is love" (1 John 4:8) and Who becomes the illumination of his heart.

27. In this struggle to cast off death-creating fear, we face the assault of the world which, bearing the marks of our sin, ever battles against our spiritual growth. This world constantly cries: "Be afraid!" as an instruction repeated more often than any other, like a force-fed substitute for genuine food. "Embrace fear! Accept dread!" For what do the societies of this fallen age do if not instruct man in what to fear, and whom, and how provocatively? Or what is the governing principle of our generation, if not the continual response to perpetual fear—real and imagined—in the shaping of states and cultures and societies? Man is taught to fear his brother, to fear war, to fear disease, to fear God, even to fear himself. Yet the Christian is a child of Him Who created the heavens and the earth, Who has power over darkness and death, and Who speaks

to our hearts: " Do not fear, little flock, for it is your Father's good pleasure to give you the kingdom" (Luke 12:32).

28. Here we may hear the words of the Apostle, that "perfect love casts out fear" (1 John 4:18). This becomes the entry-point to spiritual knowledge, for such knowledge begins with love and is governed by it. This is a love that shows up fear as the fruit of the "father of lies" (cf. John 8:44) and cleanses man's heart from the scourge of his intellectual darkness. Perfect love grounds the beginning of the ascent of knowledge in truth, rather than a lie; in clarity of vision, rather than blindness.

29. Fear, by contrast, begins with confusion and shores up slavery. A man who is free in Christ is not afraid, because the full measure of his life is summed up in the One Who has tasted death and prevailed, Who has entered Hades and emerged from its shattered gates victorious. But a confused man finds himself shackled not to Christ but to his own thoughts and concerns, which enslave him in the depths of the Hades of his own anguish.

30. We speak here not of the pure fear of the Lord, which itself is completely imbued with love and which the Holy Scriptures tell us abides forever and even command us always to retain, saying: "Serve the Lord in fear, and rejoice unto Him with trembling" (Ps 2:11). Rather, we speak of what St Philaret calls "slavish fear," from which the Christian must in due course be purified.[53] Here, as in many things, the Holy Fathers guide us in understanding aright the distinction of things that may have a common name, since they are generally taken to be one and the same, but which in fact are as utterly different as night and day. There is true love just as there is false love (for self-love is commonly called "love,"

even though in reality it is not love at all), and so, too, there is Godly fear and ungodly; moreover, there is also a Godly fear which is good "in its season" (cf. Ps 1:3) but must ultimately be overcome, and a Godly fear that should abide perpetually.

31. Slavish fear fits into the category of a fear that can be good, so long as it does not become worldly, but in any case must not abide forever. Fear of the consequences of breaking the divine commandments, for example, can have a positive purpose, especially at the beginning of the spiritual ascent, helping man discern between right and wrong and bear fruits in his interior growth; precisely such fear "is the beginning of wisdom" (Prov 1:7). It is also precisely the kind of fear that must be "cast out" by perfect love, in due measure, for what is born of the fear of consequences matures into love that acts not out of a desire to avoid repercussions, but to cling to the object of its love.[54] Thus such "slavish fear" can have its place and lead to good; yet such fear is wholly distinct from the fear engendered by the world—for worldly fear does not place one on the path to love, but to despair. It darkens the intellect and chills the soul.

32. Worldly fear is never the beginning of wisdom nor its "crown" (cf. Sir 1:16). It is not the fear that causes a man's soul to "dwell at ease" nor which opens his heart to receive the "Law in the way which He hath chosen" (Ps 24:12–13 LXX). It is the barren embrace of hopelessness; it leads away from God, not toward Him.

33. Worldly fear is the stultification of the ascent toward Life. It is the crippling of a soul that would attain to divine things, binding it instead to the earthly; and worse, to that which is most base in the distortion of earthly things.

34. If you are unsure of the nature of the fear that is in you, test it by its offspring. Worldly fear gives birth to despair, anxiety, despondency, and the swelling of the passions. Godly fear, by contrast, gives birth to a state of confidence in the Divine Will, a burning desire to do good and to live according to God's purposes, and a growing trust in the power of the Author of Life to conquer the death within and around us.

35. Beware when the world attempts to teach you what to fear, and whom, and how: the real concern is not with the supposed objects of such fear (which, in any case, are never stronger than the power of God to make good of them), but of the fact that such fear will quell the stirrings of love within you. The objects of worldly fear will still be conquered by the might of God; but you will have led yourself to defeat if you permit worldly fear to become your master.

36. When the ascent toward Love is thwarted in the heart, so too is the ascent toward knowledge. A man bound by the chains of worldly fear can never know God truly, nor himself, nor the world around him. Do not, therefore, willingly allow yourself to be made a fool by permitting fear to render you witless.

37. So much of the world's spiritual and moral confusion stems from this willing admission of the opposite of true intellectual clarity into man's heart. The man cowering in fear will always be confused as to the authentic realities of life; and the greater his fear, the greater his confusion.

38. Such confusion makes it difficult, often impossible, to discern reality, even when faced with it directly. This is what Christ and the Fathers refer to as spiritual blindness: the inability to

perceive truth, even when standing before it, face to face. Such is epitomized in the words of Pilate, who, standing before Truth incarnate, looked into His eyes and demanded, "What is truth?" (John 18:38), thus becoming a perpetual image of a man with eyes, but who does not see (cf. Mark 8:18; Jer 5:21)—and this, precisely because he was bound by worldly fear (cf. John 19:8, 12–13).

39. Yet blindness can come also from a more innocent ignorance, which arises not from a willful submission to fear, but from the lack of training in the *nous* that renders spiritual eyes open and alert. Thus did some of our Holy Fathers perceive the condition of our first parents: the confusion of Adam and Eve over heeding the Lord's commandment, which was cunningly manipulated by the serpent, was not motivated by a willful desire for evil nor the crippling effects of worldly fear (for this would fall upon them only later), but an inexperience in obedience that the devil used to mislead them, which St Irenaeus calls a "neglect."[55]

40. The Righteous Prophet Samuel did not rightly perceive the voice of the Lord when it came to him at Shiloh, mistaking it for the voice of Eli, his elder and priest (cf. 1 Kgdms 3:2–14), and so the tender call of the Holy God of Israel stirred confusion in his heart. How much more ignorant is a man's soul, which does not know or even seek the voice of the Lord! How his confusion reigns, so that he seeks among men that which has its only true source in God. For this brother we must pray, that he be given ears to comprehend, and may say also to our Saviour in due course: "Speak Lord, for" at last "Thy servant hears" (cf. 1 Kgdms 3:9–10).

41. As young Samuel "did not yet know the Lord, and the word of the Lord had not yet been revealed to him" (cf. 1 Kgdms 3:7),

he required a teacher who might guide him into the discernment required to respond aright to the Divine Voice. We, too, must implore the Lord that He grant us also a sure instructor in the Faith, who may "perceive that the Lord is calling" (1 Kgdms 3:8) and instruct us with power, both what to do and what to say.

42. Some may say, there is no man to guide me, on account of my weakness and the laxity of this present generation. If so, let him pray thus: "Do Thou Thyself be my Teacher, O my Saviour! Not through my seeking of any private illumination or the sore delusion that alone I can learn or know Thy Will—God, forbid such pretension!—but, rather, in Thy Church guide me to the true purpose of this created life." As once wrote Elder Nectarius of Optina, "One must know the purpose of life to be free,"[56] so may the Lord set free a man through heartfelt obedience to His Holy Church, that he may love God all his days without ungodly fear.

43. "Faith in the truth saves; faith in a lie and in diabolic delusion is ruinous;"[57] thus the Christian is taught that ungodly fear arises when his heart is led into confusion and deception. But let him not despair, if his surroundings appear a shambles and poor soil for the growth of the spirit: for "as our guide ... we have been given by God Himself the Law of God ... and the tradition of the Church."[58] From this banquet the faithful man knows he shall receive food sufficient for the salvation of his soul.

44. Some may stand in want of eldership, some of the means of instruction they self-willfully define as their "necessity;" but none who would submit themselves before her stands in want of the Church, which is man's sure guide and instructor, the illumination of the elders and the teacher of our teachers.

45. The Church unerringly leads man to Truth, for she is Truth's Body and has Him as her head. For one who seeks spiritual knowledge, she is an unfailing instructor, and she provides what the world cannot give.

46. Be resolved, therefore, no more to fear the world, or death, or the powers of the evil one, or sin itself, so long as the Lord is with you. We have heard it said that "man must himself begin to desire and to seek, and then Grace will not desert him, so long as he continues to trust in it"[59]; so let our hearts be pledged to this task "from this day, from this hour, from this very moment."[60] Only pray that the Lord will guide and help and comfort us, that pious fear may approach maturity and be transformed into the love that produces wisdom and leads to spiritual knowledge.

47. The transformation from fear into love, and love into wisdom, arises from the Christian's crucifixion of heart. As he has been "baptized into Christ" (Gal 3:27), so has he been baptized into Christ's death. Only in this way is he united to the Lord's resurrection. Therefore, the interior embrace of the crucifixion is a necessary dimension of his spiritual ascent.

48. Only a crucified heart beholds the fullness of the love of God and gains real wisdom thereby. A heart that is unbroken does not feel within itself the wounds of the Saviour. It cannot wholly know the love that is broken by death and healed by resurrection.

49. When the elder and seer spoke to the Theotokos those foreboding words of love, "A sword will pierce through your own soul also" (Luke 2:35), he spoke to all generations in the person of her who is blessed of all generations (cf. Luke 1:48). The glorious descent of the Spirit, Who imbued Life in the womb of

the Mother of God, Who breathes life into the heart of every man, thrusts the spear of sacrifice into the very flesh He sanctifies. For there is no Christ to Whom we can be united except the crucified Christ; no God we can adore but the self-sacrificing God.

50. Do you wish to obtain the joy that defeats all sorrow? Do you wish to know the rejoicing that causes babes to leap and dance within the womb (cf. Luke 1:41) and all of earth and heaven to sing (cf. Ps 95:1, 11 LXX)? Then open your heart to the wounds of love. Do not flee from them! Let the sword that pierced the Mother of God's heart pierce yours in like manner; do not resist or run from it. Weep as she wept, then join her in the unending joy of the resurrection of her Son.

51. There is no God but the crucified God. There is no Christian heart but the crucified heart.

52. Remember the words of Elder Barsanuphius of the desert: "Every gift is received through pain of heart."[61] Call these words to mind especially when you feel the urge to complain about the struggles of your lot, for by such complaining you inadvertently seek to cast away the very Grace that might save you.

53. When we feel that the cup of suffering from which we have been given to drink is too deep, when its draught has been offered to us too long, we must remember that the One Who pours forth this drink is Christ, Who knows what is beneficial to us, and in what measure. Recall the words of St Ignatius: "The Heavenly Father is almighty and all-seeing. He sees your affliction, and if He had found it necessary or profitable to withdraw the cup from you, He would certainly have done so."[62]

54. Even the great St Anthony needed to be taught this spiritual lesson, after so many long years of the fiercest temptation and solitary toil in the desert. At the culmination of his great tribulation he was at last consoled by divine help that came in a bright light, and the cessation of his bodily pain; and "getting his breath again and being freed from pain, he besought the vision that had appeared to him, saying, 'Where were you? Why did you not appear at the beginning to make my pains to cease?' And a voice came to him, 'Anthony, I was here, but I waited to see your contest.'"[63] Had he not endured, how much would he have lost! Not only in his knowledge of God, but in his participation in God's Grace. For St Athanasius records that, having heard this, "Anthony arose and prayed, and received such strength that he perceived that he had more power in his body than ever before."[64]

55. Do you wish likewise to be made strong, and to acquire such power within you? It is the gift that God desires to give all His creatures. But to receive it, you must be prepared to make yourself ready through the ascesis of endurance, especially embracing suffering. It is impossible to list the multitude of saints who have borne witness across the ages that this is the key that opens such doors.

56. Too much of man's life is spent fleeing suffering, fleeing sorrow. He runs from these as from things evil and to be despised. Yet our Lord did not flee from suffering, but embraced it. He did not lament sorrow as contrary to life; rather, He beheld His friend and "wept" (John 11:35)—our human Saviour weeping His divine tears—and then that Divine-Human One raised His friend from death to life.

57. Lazarus' sisters joined our Lord in His tears. How the tender hearts of Mary and Martha broke at the loss of their beloved. Who can imagine the sorrow they bore in their souls! Who can explain such grief! And yet it was through their tears, and not apart from them, that they heard the thunderous words of the Saviour, spoken in intimate gentleness: "Lazarus, come forth!" (John 11:43). The Lord revealed His power, and they beheld the resurrection He would soon bestow on all the world. Their tears watered the earth, and it brought forth joy in place of grief; for Christ had come, as St Romanos recounts it, to "take pity, as the Merciful One, on the tears of Mary and Martha."[65]

58. If, as we have received from our Fathers, "the man who is sent unceasing sorrow is known to be especially under God's care,"[66] what fear ought there be in seeing sorrow or suffering on the horizons of our lives? Whether it be brought by illness, or loss, or circumstance: behold! The rich harvest of sorrows is blessed for Him who by faith turns sorrow into joy.

59. In the desert it was said to one who sought to avoid sorrows, that the Saviour "has allowed you to sorrow a little, so that for patience you might receive from Him mercy," and again, "our Master entered for us all sufferings: why then do not we, remembering them, endure, so as to become communicants of them?"[67] Have you a better answer to this than the silence which greeted the elder's question? Accept in gratitude the sufferings that draw you into communion with Christ: do not fear them!

60. Suffering is both joy- and wisdom-creating. He who freely accepts sorrow and does not despair, receives by this very disposition the keys to the storehouse of divine knowledge.

61. Blessed is the man who accepts this cross as the means of growth. Truly, he shall hear spoken within his heart the words the crucified Lord spoke to the repentant thief: "Today you will be with Me in Paradise" (Luke 23:43).

62. How do we crucify the heart? Begin by releasing the clutch we hold over it. Foolish man, you think your heart is yours! And so you try to guard and preserve it selfishly. Cease this at once. Make no more excuses. Give what you think is yours to the One to Whom it truly belongs, and let Him sacrifice it on the altar of His merciful love.

63. "To rest is the same as to retreat."[68] Such council must always be with you in your quest to transform your heart. This heart cannot be given to God unless you are willing to act: to release your clutch over it, to unbind it from the world, and to hand it to the God of mercy.

64. In this task, you may find it beneficial to pray like this: "Lord, I am weak: help me to trust Thee. Lord, I am frail: give me strength to follow Thee. Lord, I am downcast: resurrect my heart to love Thee. Lord, I know only my sin: give me hope to know also Thy forgiveness and compassion." "Restore unto me the joy of Thy salvation" (Ps 51:12 NKJV), that I may serve Thee all my days with purity of heart.

65. "At times I fear, in my mourning, that Thou hast cast me away, O Lord, for I have so grievously sinned against Thee. I know my heart and it is wicked and vile; yet Thou hast permitted me to see into the mystery of Thy mercy. Thy love has made the adulterous woman whole (cf. John 7:53–8:11), has cured Mary of her seven demons (cf. Luke 8:2) and has made the

defiled one pure (cf. Matt 9:20–22). So cleanse my heart, also, most merciful Saviour, and do not forget me, Thy wayward child. 'Cast me not away from Thy presence, and take not Thy Holy Spirit from me' (Ps 50:13 LXX), but cling to me in love, who am unworthy of love, and grant me a new heart to serve Thee."

66. "Though I am weak I cannot despair, for I worship the Living God. Though my sinful thoughts are more in number than the sands of the sea (cf. Ps 138:18 LXX) and I have fallen from a child of light to a child of darkness, there shines yet in this darkness the Unconquerable Light. Thy Cross is my vision and hope—that Tree which defeated Hades, and which has the power to conquer my own sin, also."

67. Are you afraid to enter more deeply into the life of repentance, which leads to love, which leads to knowledge, because you fear the power of the evil one and his cunning? The divinely experienced Elder Joseph also knew this temptation, and the Lord revealed to him the counsel to combat it: "Stand up. Get angry with the tempter, knowing that he is the one that contrives trickery. Do not let him get away with it—fight him!"[69] And again, "Do not despair … but once again rise, repent, and weep."[70]

68. Thus ever arising, the devil is given no place in the heart, and the doors that he has cruelly fastened shut may by divine power be opened. Then it behoves us to pray with conviction the prayer of St Dimitri of Rostov: "Open, O doors and bolts of my heart, that Christ the King of Glory may enter! Enter, O my Light, and enlighten my darkness; enter O my Life, and resurrect my deadness!"[71] And the Lord truly enters, and the Spirit, and the Father's creature is given the strength to rise up yet higher.

69. Persistence in the spiritual struggle is essential to the attainment of any growth. In our modern world, we see a generation brought up in the myth of instant knowledge and fragmentary wisdom; but the elements that comprise this myth are themselves falsehoods. Instant wisdom is actually foolishness; and wisdom, in fragments, divides the soul rather than unites it to a higher truth.

70. How do we see this in our day? Let us give but one example, directly related to our quest to draw closer to our Fathers' wisdom. Technological advances have made translations of the Holy Fathers and access to their sacred writings more easily available than at any point in history; but do people know the Fathers any better as a result? Rather, do we not see that all and sundry quote from the Fathers—extracted sentences here and there, devoid of any approach to those Fathers' lives, which is a necessary ingredient in understanding them? Or to an ascetical discipline, which is an absolute requirement for perceiving the meaning of such words?

71. In previous generations, to be able to adopt the Fathers' words required, at the very minimum, years (if not a lifetime) of reading through their works as wholes—there was rarely any other way. Those who adopted their words and conveyed them with authority not only spent years in such reading, but in conforming their lives to the witness of the Fathers they read, such that they gained an intimacy not only with their saintly texts, but strove to be imitators of their sanctified way of living. Then, and only then, could they take up the divine words of the Fathers and convey them with spiritual wisdom and authority.

72. This is what it means to encounter men and women who speak "with authority": namely, that the content of their words is vivified by the spiritual fortitude of their lives. They do not merely offer an artfully crafted repetition of texts and traditions; rather, they offer lives of repentant ascent in which such words are renewed for us through the same illumination that inspired their original writing. One man may quote the words of a saint with no authority to his speech, because he is merely echoing another's verbiage; while a second man may quote the same words, and in his mouth they become sharp swords that pierce the hard hearts of his hearers and spur them to new life. The difference lies not in the words, but in the life of repentance and illumination of the one who speaks them.

73. Today, however, the texts of the Holy Fathers are picked apart like meat from a carcass, torn away from the spiritual life that produced them for whatever immediate purpose one holds as relevant, hungering with the self-perceived need to adopt their tongue. And those who tear a strip of this flesh away and hold it up, feel that by doing so they demonstrate the wisdom of the Fathers, or convey the Fathers' authority. But this is a mockery of the saints, not a veneration of them.

74. Nothing could be more distant from the example of the Holy Fathers themselves, than dissecting their words for personal or ideological ends, apart from the deliberate striving to attain the same life as they had, in perfect spiritual obedience to the Church they knew as mother.

75. Nor can the wisdom of the Fathers ever be attained, much less demonstrated, merely by quoting their words. Such is an intellectual myth of modernity. Words—be they the words of the

Holy Fathers, or of the Scriptures or even of Christ Himself—can be heard countless different ways and can be presented to mean countless different things. The Church's condemnation of the absurd notion of "sola scriptura" has always conveyed this clearly. No words "speak for themselves"; rather, words are given life through their living inheritance.

76. This reality is manifested so often and so clearly that in other times it might not even need to be mentioned; but in our era, so degenerate of understanding, it is essential that it be clarified. When Christ commands His disciples to heed the second great commandment, "Love thy neighbor," one might be tempted to say that this is a "self-explanatory word" (cf. Matt 22:39). Yet it is clear even in the Gospel itself that not only was the meaning of this commandment unclear to the Lord's hearers, but even the individual concepts within it were not rightly perceived by them. The lawyer asks Christ, "And who is my neighbor?" (Luke 10:29), making it evident that this "straightforward" category could mean many things, and could be manipulated to mean many others; and it would later be clear that the disciples fundamentally misunderstood also what "love" must mean in such a commandment—until they saw Love fully manifested on the Cross and in the empty tomb.

77. The confusion generated by "self-evident" meanings of such words is not a purely ancient phenomenon. Behold how debased is the vision of "love" that is embraced by modern society! Today man readily claims he "loves his neighbor," while pouring out the greatest of evils upon him.

78. The same reality holds true with respect to the words of the Holy Fathers. Today a man thinks that if he can offer a

quotation from this Father or that one, he possesses the knowledge of the saints; but the idea that the more patristic or Scriptural writings one can summon to quote in response to any given situation equates to spiritual maturity or pious wisdom, is refuted by the devil himself, who quotes the prophets and cites the words of Scripture, yet in so doing reveals himself not as a teacher of truth but "a liar, and the father of [lies]" (John 8:44).[72] Simply quoting words is not a demonstration of knowledge of the truth.

79. The better path to knowing the Fathers, and to receiving from them guidance on the ascent to spiritual knowledge, is so to imbue oneself with their witness that one is propelled into their lives—attaining the mystical participation of a spiritual descendent.

80. To know the Holy Fathers is to live as they lived, believe as they believed, and repent as they demonstrate the path and fruits of repentance. This knowledge does not consist solely in knowing their words, but gaining their hearts; and sharing it does not consist chiefly in citing their works, but in becoming a demonstration of their lives.

81. To be sure, being intimately familiar with the actual words of the Fathers is essential. It is how we come to know them, at least in the first steps, and to be shaped by them. But if we end up only knowing their words, and do not permit those words to transform our lives, then they will not fulfill in us the power the Spirit has given them.

82. Do you see how, in this, we discover again the same truth we have discussed before? Just as spiritual knowledge is a communion

in knowledge given by the Spirit, so "patristic knowledge," if we may employ such a phrase, is knowledge given by the Fathers. A degree of knowledge can come by striving intellectually to assess their words and legacy, yes; but far higher is the knowledge that comes through a communion, in the Church, with the Fathers themselves. The saints, who are alive in Christ, are ever ready to guide us in this relationship of understanding.

83. Our approach to knowledge in the saints is therefore distinct from the purely worldly approach to the same: we do not merely analyze what they have said before, recorded in the annals of history, but we listen as they speak to us ever and always in the Church; and our ears are prepared for the hearing of their voices by the comportment of our lives.

84. It is when the saints speak to the heart that we come to know the Holy Fathers; and it is by readying the heart for that encounter through repentance and a full life in the Church that we render ourselves open to such spiritual illumination.

85. Spiritual knowledge, in this as in so many aspects, is fulfilled in action. Wisdom that does not bear fruit is barren, and a barren fruit tree is worthless, ready only to be cast away. Abject intellectualism is just such a barren tree, for it seeks wisdom for wisdom's sake; but the right use of the intellect, by contrast, is a tree that produces much fruit, for it leads to spiritual knowledge that shapes and transforms a human life.

86. The Spirit is life-bearing: knowledge that does not lead to an increase of spiritual life is not of the Spirit. Let this be another test of true knowledge. If it does not provoke a more active spiritual life, it is not spiritual knowledge.

87. The Spirit sanctifies and transforms man: knowledge that does not transform him who attains it is not of the Spirit. This is yet another test.

88. But do not grieve if the wisdom you presently possess is not yet of this highest sort. We grow in this life, and make ascent one step at a time. Do not despair if you find yourself far from the highest rung; rather, resolve to seek to ascend higher, intent to claim what is right and true. The Spirit is sought by those who crave the transfiguration He brings, and this seeking bears fruit. When the young Nikolai walked with St Seraphim in the forest, he sought the Spirit, and to be changed by Him—and the result is well known to us.[73] He can be contrasted with a man who seeks "spiritual" knowledge, but without the intention to be utterly transformed by its attainment. Such a one will never attain what he seeks. Or rather, he will attain precisely what he seeks: for in reality he does not seek the Spirit or a spiritual life at all, but only the confirmation of his mental desires.

89. The ascent of knowledge is an ever-increasing ascent of humility. Only an empty vessel can be filled; that which is filled already with its own self-understandings will retain these, remaining incapable of receiving higher things.

90. A contrast between worldly wisdom and spiritual wisdom can be discerned in this: worldly wisdom fosters in its possessor a self-confidence and increasing closed-mindedness; spiritual wisdom creates a humility that makes a heart open to the stirrings of the Spirit, relying ever less on itself and more directly clinging to the Grace of God.

91. Spiritual knowledge creates a new man out of the old (cf. Eph 4:22; 2 Cor 5:17) and brings a new birth to one

already born (cf. John 3:5). It does not transform the intellect alone, but the entirety of the human creature.

92. In this, true knowledge finds its place within the whole of the Christian mystery; for Christianity is a life, not just a way of living. It is not an orientation of life, but Life itself.

93. The demands of Christianity, and its promises, are therefore not laid solely upon our intellect or our reason, but upon the whole of our being (of which these are a sacred part). The Lord, in the entire Gospel of His saving incarnation, did not once utter, "Go ye therefore and think," but "Go and do" (cf. Luke 10:37; John 8:11). Indeed, when the Saviour speaks of the way those around Him *think*, it is overwhelmingly in critical terms. "Do not think to say to yourselves, 'We have Abraham as our father'" (Matt 3:9); "do not think that I came to destroy the Law" (Matt 5:17); "the Son of Man is coming at an hour you do not expect" (Luke 12:40); "you search the Scriptures, for in them you think you have eternal life" (John 5:39). Woe befalls men who feel that in their thoughts, life and truth are bestowed. It was to the piously educated as well as the masses that the high priest Caiaphas once asked, "What do you think" of the Christ? and "they answered and said, 'He is deserving of death'" (Matt 26:66).

94. Christ, by contrast, showed His disciples not a way of thinking or reasoning, but a life. In this life were all things: hope, healing, reason, redemption, ritual, freedom. Everything was incorporated in this life because the life itself was His. That which the Apostles and others first began to experience in its fullness was life *in Christ*, bound up in Him, united to Him—"for as many of you as were baptized into Christ have put on Christ" (Gal 3:27). A life which is united to Christ is one in which the characteristics

of Christ become man's. He Who said "I am the way, the truth, and the life" (John 14:6) is the very One Whom the Christian finds living within himself, and in Whom the Christian lives in turn. The Lord's *way*—the life of perfect obedience to the Will of the Father—becomes man's way. The One who once stood before Pilate, not as a spoken but rather the living answer to that dreadful question, "What is truth?" (John 18:38), becomes the truth, reason and enlightenment of each Christian. The same Life that conquered sin and death, which stomped upon the devil and broke the gates of Hades, is the Life into which the weak creature is borne.

95. It is this that comes to man in the ascent of knowledge. The illumination that comes from above lifts up the creature on earth below. In the illumined heart, heaven and earth meet. The creature becomes fully Christ's, no longer solely as a question of creation or origin, but of union.

96. Thus the human creature ought ever to seek after spiritual knowledge, for it is a sacramental reality that lifts him into new life.

97. Be assured, too, that this knowledge is a gift the Lord desires for you. For spiritual knowledge is communion in God Himself, and God in every age has revealed Himself as One Who desires to be source of such communion. He is the Giver Who is also the Given, the Bestower Who is also the Bestowed[74]—and the one to whom He wishes to give Himself is you.

98. So, Christian, seek wisdom and learn to love it. Climb the ladder of knowledge that the Lord has provided, learning to love what is worthy of love and to honor what is true and abiding.

Let creation be the book that you read, and your heart be the lens through which you read it, purifying that lens so that it sees more and more; and the God Who made creation will give your eyes new power, so that in due course you can see Him anew, and receive Him anew, and rise up to the heights to which He calls you.

99. God has, in Christ, made us ready to know Him fully. Let us have no higher aim!

100. To the Lord, eternal and ever-wise, who gives spiritual sight and wisdom to His creatures, be glory forever and ever: Amen!

IV

A Century on the Church

1. How can we speak of spiritual ascent or any spiritual activity at all, without speaking of the Church? For the Church is the abode of the Spirit and the sole avenue of our growth in holiness. In her, and in her alone, do we join the spiritual contest that leads to the full acquisition of the Spirit, and the race that leads to the eternal Kingdom of our Creator.

2. When in our own day we hear the great New-martyr Hilarion reminding us that "without the Church there is no salvation,"[75] he is doing naught but faithfully reiterating the testimony borne of our Fathers from the beginning. "He can no longer have God as his Father, who has not the Church as his mother," said one great lamp of the Church,[76] illumining the truth preserved from the first in our Scriptures: that "wide is the gate and broad is the way that leads to destruction, and there are many who go in by it. Because narrow is the gate and difficult is the way which leads to life" (Matt 7:13–14).

3. That narrow way is singular, as the Body of the singular true God. There is one Church and one Cup,[77] one Name under

heaven that leads to salvation (cf. Acts 4:12), and one path into Paradise, which is Christ Himself.

4. He who confesses many churches, confesses many gods. Either that, or he does not confess the Church at all, since what he calls "the church" is a thing separable from God, and therefore little more than a human invention.

5. But "God is not mocked" (Gal 6:7), and the pretensions of those who would envisage a Church other than that which He Himself founded, of which He is Head, which is His Body and is inseparable from His divine-human life, are but the weak stirrings of the "sons of men, in whom there is no salvation" (Ps 145:3 LXX).

6. The Christian must rest in surety on the promise of Christ to His Church, that "I am with you always, even to the end of the age" (Matt 28:20), knowing with full confidence that it is precisely in His Church that He is ever present in this life, manifesting to every generation His closeness and Grace through the Holy Mysteries, and leading the repentant to the fullness of Life.

7. It is thus that we are able with faith to affirm that "all power and grace have been placed in the Church, where the elders by birth hold office, and who possess the power of baptizing, of the imposition of hands, of ordaining."[78] It is here that we find the venue for that power and grace to become operative in our lives, that by the Mysteries she bestows through her ministers, the Church may lift up and heal what is fallen in us.

8. This must be emphasized all the more stringently in our day, when the dual poisons of laxity and a darkened intellect have disposed a generation to view the Church with suspicion and

even disdain; and the darts of self-gratification and ambition have moved others to view her as a thing to be grasped and manipulated.

9. But the Church remains our Mother: she teaches, she is not taught. She guides the race of man, she is not guided by it. She bestows salvation upon the world, she does not receive her being from the world's design or its desires.

10. The Church is no mere "human institution," as we hear too often in this perverse age. Fallen man so often assesses that the only things that exist are those he has contrived; and so, he determines, the Church must also be. But the Church is, rather, a mystical reality in which divine life and human life are intermingled. Her origin is not in man but in God-made-man.

11. Into her the human creature is grafted through Holy Baptism. The human element of the Church is thus present by adoption, not by foundation. Man has not created the Church; rather, it is he who finds his own creation fully realized only within her.

12. Our new birth into the Church is thus the taking up of our life into the life of God. Through Baptism, we are not merely joined to a pious human community of faith: we are drawn into the very life of Him toward Whom all true faith is directed.

13. Such life in the Church constitutes man's perpetual experience of the incarnation of the Son: for as He took flesh in order to unite it to Himself and sanctify it, so in the Church our humanity is ever taken up into this same Christ's life, sanctified through that union.[79]

14. Thus as we behold the Church, and the human creature united in her to the being of God, we see fulfilled the sacred vision

of our Holy Father: "There is a new wonder in heaven and on earth: God is on earth and man is in heaven. He united men and angels so as to bestow deification on all creation."[80]

15. The path to deification is therefore found only in this Church, for the sanctification of the creature comes not but through the union of the created with the Creator, Who is Head of the Church and the very One Who fashions that union within Himself.[81] The Church is the venue of man's re-creation in glory.

16. How foolish, by contrast, is the man who thinks he can climb to the heights of *theosis* without doing so within this Church![82] Vain is every worldly attempt—though these be made nevertheless in each generation—to be deified apart from God, Who, in His Church makes Himself wholly available. This is the lesson we learn from the building of the tower which took the name Babel (cf. Gen 11:1–9): even in its primordial ages, the human race in rebellion has strived to reach God without Him. But in those ancient days such efforts failed—and so, too, now.

17. Yet we have seen a greater miracle than any feat that could be attained by human ingenuity: no tower has been built to heaven, but heaven has stooped down to earth. By the clutches of greedy man God has not been grasped; but He has placed Himself into human hands, even those of His most-pure mother. The futile designs of human society have not created heaven upon the earth, despite the terrible efforts of generations of trying; but God has brought earth and heaven together in His own life, which He now bestows on us as members of His Body.

18. How much more is this than any mere human fabrication! The artistry of man has created many glorious things, but it has never fashioned God, nor His Body, nor His self-offering; nor has

any machination of our race ever made possible the grafting of the life of man into that of the eternal Lord. This was observed long ago by our sacred Father, St Athanasius, who asked: "How could this have come to pass"—that is, man's restored ability to know God—"save by the presence of the very Image of God, our Lord Jesus Christ? For by men's means it was impossible."[83] That is, man could by no means craft the substance of his salvation, whether through the invention of a religion or the affectation of any theological or philosophical rites. Salvation consists in the act of God uniting man to Himself. The Church, in which He effects this perpetually, could therefore never have a merely human foundation, for such is utterly beyond the capabilities of the creature needing redemption.

19. Knowing that man, accepting every demonic influence in his weakness, would embrace perversions of the true teachings regarding Christ as a pretext to divide the Church,[84] this same Athanasius, as a good and wise pastor of the flock entrusted to him by the Lord, demanded that the right vision of God (i.e., a correct theological perception) always be united to the Christian's vision of the Church. As she is the Lord's Body, to know this Church one must understand aright the nature of God.

20. Thus was the great Archbishop, like all faithful shepherds of the Church who emulate the care of the Good Shepherd (cf. John 10:11–18), dedicated to correct and precise theological articulation, not out of abstract intellectual interests, but stemming from the certain conviction that proper theology leads man into both the Church and Life, while improper theological articulation leads him away from the Church and her Truth, invariably toward sorrow and affliction.

21. Erroneous visions of God give birth to false churches; and these in return give birth in man's heart to faith in a false god, or at the very least, a deformed and partial conception of God as He really is. This is the reason that all the Fathers have seen theology not as an academic intellectual pursuit, but a saving pastoral necessity.

22. The right faith and teaching which come to us through the Church, and which in turn teach us about Christ's Body, are therefore essential ingredients in establishing a spiritual life. To believe wrongly is spiritually suicidal. Consciously to impose false belief is the same as to commit murder.

23. Do away, therefore, with every false thought that the vicissitudes of history have suggested, which leads to a debasement of the Church in your understanding. The Church is neither human endeavor nor historical creation; she suffers no debasement nor diminution, however many centuries she may stand in this world, for she is always and ever the Body of Christ, governed by the Father's Spirit: the manifestation in this world of the eternity of the most sacred Trinity.

24. History cannot defeat the Church, neither human weakness nor demonic rebellion. A "church" that is merely the fabrication of man—yes, such can fall, and more than this, it surely will. But the true and only Church is God's own, and God is not defeated.

25. Surely the words of the Holy Apostle Paul apply to our reflections here, when with Spiritual inspiration he writes: "I am persuaded that neither death nor life, nor angels nor principalities nor powers, nor things present nor things to come, nor height nor depth, nor any other created thing, shall be able

to separate us from the love of God which is in Christ Jesus our Lord" (Rom 8:38–39). As there is no power that might rend us from such love, so there is no power that might rend us from the Church which is the divine embodiment of that love.

26. When man speaks of the troubles that befall the Church, or the turmoils that at times rage against her, or even amongst those living within her embrace, he must understand that he speaks not of the Church in her essence, but of the frailties of the humanity that seeks its abode in her. To claim the Church as frail when those grafted into her life demonstrate their weakness is like claiming that the sun lacks strength because certain men, choosing by their deeds to cower in shadows, cannot feel its rays. Or, to employ another image: a branch grafted onto a vine may wither if it rejects the nourishment of the vine and accepts only the store of sap within itself; but its withering is not a sign of the defect of the vine, but of the branch not having been changed by that into which it was grafted, and therefore not receiving the source of abundant life beyond itself.

27. We witness the stability of the Church precisely in the fact that man's sin and weakness never thwart her; that the devil's machinations never overpower her; that even the most arrogant and cunning of foes cannot conquer that which is Christ's in this world. Man's sinful labors always fall, but the Church stands forever.

28. Hear the holy words of St Philaret of Moscow, who makes this clear: "The Church is holy, although there are sinners within her. Those who sin, but who cleanse themselves with true repentance, do not keep the Church from being holy. But unrepentant sinners are cut off, whether visibly by Church authority, or invisibly by

the judgement of God, from the Body of the Church. And so in this regard, the Church remains holy."[85] This we hear also from the tongue of St Justin: "A division within the Church has never occurred, nor indeed can one take place; while apostasy from the Church has and will continue to occur after the manner of those voluntarily fruitless branches which, having withered, fall away from the eternally living theanthropic Vine: the Lord Christ" (cf. John 15:1–7).[86]

29. Not only is the Church not deprived of her holiness on account of the sinful machinations of man, but she remains ever-undivided, despite the divisions such men seek to sow. "From time to time," our Holy Father continues, "heretics and schismatics have cut themselves off and have fallen away from the one and indivisible Church of Christ, whereby they ceased to be members of the Church and parts of her theanthropic Body. The first to fall away thus were the gnostics, then the Arians, then the Macedonians, then the Monophysites, then the iconoclasts, then the Roman Catholics, then the Protestants, then the Uniates, and so on."[87]

30. To his listing we must sorrowfully add those of more recent days who, rejecting the theological unity of the Church and her canonical tradition—which guides each generation to the preservation of unity in Truth—have cut themselves away into barren schism and heresy. In our contemporary age we cannot fail to includes those who, under various guises, adopt the neo-papal concept of a primate "without equals"[88]; those who tread upon the Holy Canons and declare heterodox to be Orthodox by personal fiat; those who place non-ordained men in clerical positions and open the poisonous jaws of deceit against the faithful who

are, in their innocence, led to believe they receive sacraments at the hands of those who are in reality merely laymen dressed up in priestly garments, at whose hands no sacraments can be performed; and those who, for lust of power and authority, stomp upon the canonical order of the Church and lay waste to the peace of the faithful. May God have mercy upon them, and on us all! But do not be deceived: even such men do not disfigure the Church, for they do not—despite such efforts—change her, but rather cut themselves off from her by their very acts. And yet there is hope for return, which must be that for which every Christian sincerely prays.

31. Indeed, it is precisely the fact that the Church is not changed by schism or heresy, but rather those who engage in it are cut away from her, that gives cause of hope for restoration. For if the errors of man were to alter the nature of the Church, or the salvific purity of her teaching, then there would be no calm harbor back into which one could return after having stirred up the waters of strife. But because error does not alter her interior state, but severs man from communion in her unthwartable purity, the Church remains a haven of potential restoration for those who have sought to do her wrong, or whose other desires may have resulted in such a sorrowful severance, but who come to themselves and seek in repentance to be restored to the Truth.

32. Yet in those moments when apostasy rears itself, when hardness of heart seems to preclude the heeding of that call to reconciliation, the comfort of the Christian resides in the sure knowledge that such sin will never—and can never—change the nature of the Church. Man, quite simply, has no power, however deep his sin or lofty his ambition, to alter the nature of Christ or His Body.

"According to her theanthropic nature," St Justin teaches, "the Church is one and unique, just as Christ the God-man is one and unique. Hence, a division, a splitting up of the Church, is ontologically and essentially impossible."[89] Man can alter and lay waste to his own heart, but not God's.

33. When, therefore, we behold what appears to be "division within the Church" or her "splitting up" at the hands of demonically inspired schism (for all division is the work of the demons), we must recognize in this that we make a purely worldly observation. In worldly terms, if one becomes two, it has been divided. But in ecclesial terms, if the one Church experiences the schism of some internal member or faction, such that after this rebellion there are two or more using the title "church," in reality there remains only one. The division is illusory. The false church born of schism is no church at all; and the true Church which is Christ's Body remains as ever before, and so unto the consummation of history.

34. On this rock, therefore, the Christian may truly stand firm and secure. Waves may crash against this rock, but they shall never break it. Rather, like the great fortifications of a sea-wall protecting a harbor, this rock breaks up those waves, so that the water beyond remains peaceful and calm, and a safe harbor for those taking refuge therein.

35. For this reason we have learned from our Fathers to speak of the Church in terms of power—she is valiant, victor, unconquerable, fortress—but also in terms of maternal tenderness. She is mother, harbor, care-giver, healer and the embrace of love. The ascent toward godliness thus has both its strength and its solace in her solid embrace.

36. The reality of Christ's incarnation, which, as we have said before, is continually experienced in His Church, is the means by which His Life becomes ours therein. In that incarnation, the world beheld the wonderful intermingling of divine and material, wrought in Christ's Person for the salvation of man: flesh and bone were united with the Bodiless; the temporal was united with the Eternal—creation was united with its Creator. And this incarnational union is the substance, in turn, of the Church's sacramental life and mission. Each Sacrament is an extension of this mystery: for Christ continues, in His Body, to sanctify creation through union with Himself, and by those sanctified means, to draw man into His Life.

37. Thus in the chief Holy Mysteries of our "putting on Christ"— that is, Holy Baptism and Chrismation, which are separate in form but unified into a singular liturgical-sacramental act in customary practice—the Lord does not abandon His incarnational work, but continues to use the elements of creation as the quickening means of bestowing His Grace. Water is taken up and sanctified, and oil, and these material elements become the means by which what is broken in man is healed through the direct encounter with the Divine.

38. This is foretold already in the Gospel, in which Christ's material incarnation (i.e., His own becoming flesh from the Virgin and living in the world of His creation) is tied to the manner of His healing of broken humankind. When the man born blind is made whole, it is not merely by word or fiat; but the Lord "spat on the ground and made clay with the saliva; and He anointed the eyes of the blind man with the clay. And He said to him, 'Go, wash in the pool of Siloam' So he went and washed, and came

back seeing" (John 9:6–7). It is surely the Lord's divine Grace that grants new physical eyes to this man who hitherto had no means of sight; and this Grace comes to him through the mud of dust and spittle that are sacred precisely because they are drawn into the divinity of Christ the God-man.

39. In making the blind man whole in this manner, healing him through mud and spittle, the Lord showed His deep love for the material handiwork of His creative endeavor; and He revealed anew that He works man's salvation not apart from that materiality, but with His own hands touching the fabric of the cosmos and rendering it both sanctified and sanctifying.

40. Likewise in Baptism and Chrismation, it is divine Grace that grafts rebellious man into the vine of Christ's life and makes him a member of the one Church; and now, as ever, Christ effects the working of this Grace in us through the mystery of His incarnation. In each baptism He again takes the physical matter of creation, unites it to Himself, and thereby heals in us both the physical and spiritual.

41. In Baptism we are washed; through Chrismation we are sealed. In Christ God our soul is touched through the body, the spirit through the flesh, and we experience in our humanity the divine power manifest by the Saviour in His.

42. We know no other Christ than this, nor any other Church than is His Body. Therefore we know no other ecclesial means of union in that Grace than those which the Lord has Himself established and set forth for us in this Body.

43. If the Sacraments are rejected, man rejects not merely rites or rituals, but the very confession of the Lord's coming in the

flesh and the divine mystery of His salvation of the human race. The pre-eternal Son of the Father does not sanctify or save man apart from taking flesh and working within man's materiality: how brazen, then, are those who in our own day would diminish the Sacraments and announce that by some *fiat* of their own personal determination, that which the Lord Himself would not do, they are ready to undertake!

44. Let us be plain and clear, in the face of the scandals that in our day so tirelessly are leveled against the truth: the only means of entry into the Church are through her Sacraments, as they have been appointed by God to draw man into her life. Do not be deceived: any other attempt is vain and a lie. He who accepts that a man can be a member of the Church by some other method or means, or by any action undertaken outside the One True Church, rather than within her or through the mystical means at her employ, by which that begun outside her is laid claim to, corrected and perfected within her, rejects the theology of the Church and therefore rebels against God, Who is her Head.

45. Christ God left no other instruction for the redemption of the world than the very charge He gave to His disciples: "Go therefore and make disciples of all the nations, baptizing them in the name of the Father and of the Son and of the Holy Spirit, teaching them to observe all things that I have commanded you" (Matt 28:19–20). "Teaching them to observe all things whatsoever I have commanded you": Christ emphasizes, in this very instruction, that His commandment regarding the necessity of Baptism, and all His other commandments are the substance of what must be the Apostles' preaching, and the foundation of their life as the pillars of His Church.

46. Such instructions—which come down therefore from Christ and His Apostles—shall always be for us the sole standards of our ecclesial life. Man's mutable understandings may change over time, his desire to bend the practices of the Church to his own predilections may ebb and flow, but we shall ever "take our stand upon the rock of faith and the tradition of the Church, neither removing the boundaries set by our Holy Fathers of old (cf. Prov 22:30 LXX), nor giving room to those who would introduce innovation and undermine the economy of the Holy Catholic and Apostolic Church of God."[90]

47. Why do we stress this so firmly here, when the object of our focus in these pages is the ascent of the spiritual life into Godliness? Because our modern generation is riven with the schismatic impulses of those who, for whatever reason, wish to reject or "revise" the teaching of the Church regarding Baptism and Chrismation, and the other Holy Mysteries, in order to accommodate their own understandings and desires. While to spiritually insensate minds such matters may seem overly technical or even political (and we cannot deny the reality of the latter realm in many of these discussions), the real fruit of such endeavors is, rather, spiritual—because it is theological. It is intimately tied to our potential for spiritual growth.

48. A man can have no authentically spiritual life if he is not grafted into the true Life of the true Christ, Who bestows upon him the Holy Spirit of His Father. True spirituality is only and ever sanctification in the Holy Spirit. All other "spiritualities" are fabrications and emulations.

49. Moreover, one who seeks a "spiritual" life that is not life in the Holy Spirit opens himself most readily to the assaults of the

demons, who, as fallen spirits, are ready and even anxious to step into a "spirituality" devoid of the pursuit of the true Spirit of God.

50. So it is that the pursuit of a spiritual life must needs be a pursuit of the ecclesial life; that is, life in the Church. It is in the Son's Name that the Father sends the Spirit (cf. John 14:16–26); therefore, to be grafted into Christ's Body is to be united to Him through Whom the Spirit is given to us, even as He promised: "I will send Him to you" (John 16:7); and even as that Spirit came like "tongues of fire" into the hearts of the Apostles and the holy women, and comes still unto us today (cf. Acts 2:1–4).

51. Do you seek a spiritual life? Do you desire the heights of spiritual knowledge and growth and love? Do you long to stand upon the divine mountaintop that is the summit of spiritual ascent, after the manner that St Gregory understood Moses's ascent of Sinai, where at last in a bright darkness He beheld the uncreated glory of God?[91] Seek these things nowhere other than in the Church, for only in her embrace will you find them.

52. The Church shall render you spiritual by imparting unto you the Holy Spirit, a gift infinitely greater than any human enterprise of esoteric spiritualizing.

53. The Church shall breathe anew into your nostrils the "breath of life," even as God so did to Adam and Eve (cf. Gen 2:7); and being vivified through communion in the Spirit, you shall be drawn into a life beyond the capabilities of dust and flesh.

54. It is through the invocation of this same Spirit that the incarnational redemption wrought by the Son is made present anew to us in the Holy Mysteries of the Church. Therefore, one who seeks the spiritual life while rejecting the Church's sacramental realities,

or thinks that it can be obtained apart from them, denies the Spirit to himself and those who might follow him.

55. The "economy"[92] by which at times our hierarchs, guided by pastoral concerns, might apply the sacramental Grace of the Church to those being united to her, is undertaken in order to prevent the brokenness of man's lot in this world from leading him to a yet more dire state; but this *economia*—which, rightly exercised, is never an alternative to canonical order but an application of the salvific truth of that order to a pressing and singular case that will then be lain upon the hierarch's soul at the last judgment—never moves the hierarch or the recipient of his compassion away from the Church's Sacraments, but toward them in a therapeutically necessary way.

56. There is no "economy," however, by which the Sacraments may be circumvented, for there is no spiritual medicine that might be given apart from the means of encountering the Grace of God. There are indeed cases when a man may be in need of union in God's Grace amidst circumstances so dire that a successor to the Holy Apostles deems appropriate a particular approach, conformable to the specific needs of this "lost sheep," in order that he not "put forth an impediment to the saved"[93] and that he, as one of the Church's pastors, "offer a treatment suited to the sin in question, lest by employing an immoderate adjustment in one direction or the other, they fail in compassing the salvation of the one who is ailing."[94] But this will never be accomplished by the one in such need being turned away thereby from the Sacraments, for these are the very medicine of his redemption! When, therefore, in our day we hear at times of *economia* being cited as a justification for a course of "pastoral care" that in fact diminishes or even abandons

the sacramental means of the Church's healing ministry, we must recognize this as a dangerous error.

57. By contrast, the right exercise of *economia* precisely reorients a man in his reception of the Sacraments. It may cause them to be effected in his particular case in a manner otherwise unusual (with respect to the cases of most), but it does so in order that the sacramental Grace might be the more wholly manifest in his life, more completely received by him, than would be the case were such pastoral measures not taken. If, however, it results in the departure from the Sacraments themselves, or in the claiming of non- or false-sacraments to be equivalent to the one Church's true and saving Sacraments (that is to say, to treat non-medicine as if it were true medicine), a man may be assured the supposed "economy" is most certainly a deficiency and not an aid.

58. By this, to be explicit, I would include the "economy" by which a man with no Church baptism is received into Orthodoxy without a sacramental foundation to that reception; or the "economy" by which a heterodox cleric is received into Orthodoxy as a "priest" without having Apostolic hands lain upon his head in the Orthodox sacrament of Ordination. I do not dare to speak in absolutist terms that would deny any possibility of God being able to wrest good out of such unusual circumstances or bestow Grace in exception in those places where His customary instructions have not been followed (and there have been cases in past and recent memory where such things have taken place, in response to the most unusual of circumstances); but the practices of our Faith are not built on the "what if?" postulations of how God might act beyond the contours of the life He has actually bestowed upon us. More concretely, the rules that govern our

lives in the Church, and our approach to spiritual healing, are not to be manufactured based on such hypotheticals, but rooted in what the Lord has clearly commanded.

59. "Is not God capable of bestowing the Grace of union in His Church without the sacrament of Baptism being performed?" is a hypothetical; "Go ye" and "baptise…" (cf. Matt 28:19) is the divine instruction Christ has actually given. "Cannot a Priest receive the charism of the Spirit without the Church's sacramental ordination rite being performed?" is a hypothetical; but "they laid hands on them, and they received the Holy Spirit" (Acts 8:17) is the actual witness of the Apostles. At some point, the Christian must ask whether he wishes to follow his hypothetical vision of what God might do, or the concrete revelation of what God has actually done; whether he seeks an apostolic life in conjecture of what the Apostles might have done, or one in the embrace of what they actually did?

60. The revelation given through that concrete witness is clear: God does not save the suffering by depriving them of His Grace, but by drawing them into it! Shall we, with that Grace at our fingertips in the Holy Mysteries, deny it to those in need?

61. At times, some might counter, is not the sacrament of Holy Baptism "bypassed" when, by the exercise of economy, a hierarch might bless an individual who enters into the Church to do so via anointing with myrrh (Chrismation) rather than Baptism? Firstly, let us say at the outset that this is done too frequently. *Economia* by definition is an exceptional pastoral act; it must never become a norm, lest we set ourselves above the Spirit-led Holy Fathers who have clearly told us what the norms are

to be. But in those cases where a hierarch deems that, following canonical principles,[95] a man or a woman may be received by the sealing with holy chrism, a right understanding of what is actually taking place is essential. The intrinsic connection between Baptism and Chrismation is here directly exposed. An individual brought into the Church in such circumstances is not chrismated "instead of" being baptized; rather, the baptism-chrismation begun partially, incompletely, outside the Church—and therefore not possibly identical or correlate to the Church's true Baptism—is taken up by this measure of economy as an impartial and fractured shell of the true Sacrament (which, by definition, it was not); and by piecing together the fragments thus present, bringing them together, as it were, with the "perfection" (fulfillment) of the baptismal rite—the Chrismation with sacred oil—it renders the individual a baptized and chrismated Christian who must thereafter have full confidence that the grounding of his sacramental life is made wholly Orthodox.

62. A right understanding of what we have said here is essential in our day. Orthodoxy does not recognize or accept the so-called sacraments of the heterodox, being unwilling to divide her faith just as she is unwilling (to press the metaphor) to divide her God. The economy of reception by Chrismation is not a recognition of a "valid" sacrament of baptism performed by the non-Orthodox (for "it is not Baptism that the heretics are practicing"[96]); rather, it is a reclamation of that begun outside the Church, drawing it into herself and, sacramentally, reclaiming it for Holy Orthodoxy and making it real, effective and perfect, culminating in the oil of Chrismation. The heterodox quasi-baptism is thus rendered Orthodox precisely through the economy of its reclamation

and transformation within the true Church. It becomes a true Sacrament by being brought into, corrected, and made whole by the Church of the Sacraments.

63. Thus the economy of reception into Orthodoxy by Chrismation, which we repeat should be a rarity and only ever exercised in adherence to clear canonical principles, is in reality a confirmation precisely of the fact that the Church does *not* recognize the so-called sacraments of heterodox confessions— nor that she accepts this one while rejecting others, as we sometimes hear erroneously maintained. By perfecting a foreign rite, that rite is at one and the same time clearly confessed as imperfect and wanting. Or, to put this more succinctly: by submitting the beginnings of the baptismal-charismatic action to the corrective Grace of its perfection, the beginnings are confessed as insufficient, yet redeemable through incorporation into the Grace-filled reality of the true Church.

64. Those, however, who claim that the principle of economy, with respect to the making Orthodox of an individual, can be extended to other Holy Sacraments—suggesting, for example, that a non-Orthodox individual might enter into the life of the Church simply through partaking of Holy Communion, or Confession, or clerical concelebration—can only appear to us to err greatly. We simply do not find, in the Apostolic teaching of the Church, any witness to these Sacraments being employed as the means of entry into her fold (though she at times employs them as a means of receiving *back* those who were already in the Church but who were enticed away by schism or heresy, then repented and sought return[97]). The sole means of entry *into* the Church, which we have received from the Apostles, is the Mystery of

Baptism-Chrismation, by which a man has access to the other sacred Mysteries. This has been the teaching and the practice of the Church since the commandment was thus given by Christ Himself.

65. The situation of renovationist sacramentality "by economy" becomes all the more pastorally dire when a man ordained in a heterodox context is received into Orthodoxy as a Priest, without receiving the Apostolic laying on of hands and the Church's ordination to the Holy Priesthood. Once again, delving into the realm of hypotheticals is a temptation some find hard to resist. Cannot God render priestly a man who has not undergone the normal route of ordination as Priest? Does not the Lord have the power to do this exceptional thing? It would be foolish for anyone to claim a limit to God's power, or to pretend to know what He can or cannot do; yet the teaching of the Church on this matter is clear and ancient. Ordination is through the laying on of hands. Explicitly, the Church instructs that those who were clerics outside the Church are to be received as laymen, though even in ancient times there were those who, as today, "still cling to their ordination for its esteem,"[98] despite the Church's clear proclamation that, if it be established that the ordination of a man "has been performed by heretics," he must, on entering the true Church, be truly ordained—"for those who have been baptised or ordained by such persons cannot possibly be either faithful Christians or clergymen."[99]

66. Again, you may here ask, why do we stress this in our discussion of spiritual ascent? But as we have emphasized the importance of the Church as the avenue of spiritual growth, and the impossibility of attaining such growth apart from her, so we must

stress this necessary correlate of the Church's true Priesthood. As the Church effects the transformation of man through the Grace of the Sacraments, her legitimate Priesthood is a necessity in fulfilling this mission to the "lost sheep" (cf. Luke 15:3–7). Only a true priest may do that which Christ Himself commands and enables of the Priesthood; any other is an imitator engaged in pantomime. For if a man who has never received the Grace of the Holy Spirit through the laying on of hands goes about "celebrating the sacraments," what is he really doing? It cannot be the enacting or bestowing of a Grace he has not himself received; it cannot be the expression of an anointing he has not been given. It can be but a shadow, not the light; a ritualized fabrication, not the embodiment of a Divine Mystery. This is true of one who has never received the Grace of this anointing through ordination, as it is also of one who departs from the canonical life of the Orthodox Priesthood and thus finds that Grace withdrawn. An individual's proclamation of priestly status cannot replace the Grace of God, nor can any other's claim of affirmation or acceptance of it. The Priesthood is not merely an intellectual or administrative declaration: it is a charismatic reality of sacramental Grace received, exercised, and conveyed.

67. We by no means wish to condemn or cast into doubt the personal sincerity of those who bear the title "priest" as bestowed through some context other than the Orthodox Church's sacramental ordination; but piety demands that we affirm this is something other than the Church's Priesthood. The Priesthood is not a decision of men or of institutions: it is the anointing with Priestly Grace by God in His Church.

68. It behoves the Christian therefore to be watchful. True spiritual ascent, gained through the sacramental life of the Church,

cannot be obtained from the hands of those who cannot bestow it. Beware, therefore, lest you be deceived.

69. In all that we have said above, let it be clear that we have been speaking of those who come to Orthodoxy from outside the Church, whether having the origin of their religious life in a heterodoxy marked by schism, heresy, or indifference. There is a different manner of reception that applies to those who began within the Church, having been baptised and chrismated within Holy Orthodoxy, and in some cases also ordained therein, but who departed into schism. In their cases, the Holy Fathers have guided us to receive them back in relation to the measure and manner of their rebellion, which can in some cases mean through Holy Confession.[100] But this is not an exception to what we have said above; it is precisely because such persons have received the sacramental foundation of Holy Baptism and Chrismation in the Church, that their return back to her from a degree of rebellion can stand upon those sacramental foundations still present—if, indeed, buried deep under the mire of apostasy—and by the other Sacraments reclaim those present foundations unto new life. But one cannot return to that from which one has not departed; one cannot wash away the mud from a gem he has never possessed. Thus the Church faithfully maintains these distinctions, so that in her there is never found a deceit of Grace, nor are the faithful exposed to falsehood and pretension.

70. Thus preserved in her sacramental identity, the Church provides for broken man a means to be refashioned unto Life. It is the same Creator Who originally fashioned the human creature from the dust, Who in the Sacraments recreates what had been disfigured. We, who are made after the Image of Father—that is, the Son—are refreshed in that image when the Image Himself comes

to us. Through sacramental Grace, image meets Image and finds the means of its restoration.

71. The Church thus provides the human creature the means of return to its first-created state, which is a readiness to grow into the glory of God. For man, fashioned after the Image of God, was always meant to grow into that likeness in which he had first been established—the likeness of the incarnate Son of the Father.

72. Where for ages man has stumbled through history, his feet heavy upon the earth, weighed down by the consequences of his sin, in the Church He is made a new communicant in the Paradise from which he had been cast (cf. Gen 3:24), in order that he again may walk the straight path into eternity.

73. The food for which Adam longed, but which he had not yet attained the maturity to eat, is made available to us in the Church: the very Tree of Life (cf. Gen 2:9, 3:22–24), which is Christ's precious Cross, imparts Life to the world and bestows the knowledge of good and evil into the heart of man who attains maturity in His Life.

74. Entering into this Paradise in which the Tree of Life stands ever at its center and the fullness of Life is made the object of not only man's veneration but also his communion and union, that which is spiritual in him is directly fed. Each Holy Mystery brings precisely this Grace: communion in the Tree of Life and the One Whose life it bestows.

75. Every Sacrament is theological and creative. Theological, because it exposes man directly to God; and creative, because it perfects creation in a human life, through creation itself.

76. Moreover, the sacramental Grace of the Church extends beyond the momentary boundaries of the Holy Sacraments themselves. It is the same Grace that infuses the whole life of the Church, into which the Christian is grafted; and so this Grace may sanctify the entirety of his life also. All has the potential to impart God's Life to us; all might become sacramental.

77. In the Church, the whole scope of our worshiping life becomes the means of spiritual ascent: every sacred rite, every holy icon, every word and theological hymn, every action and movement. All are sanctified by the Grace of Him Whose Body the Church is, and by this Grace what otherwise might be mere gestures or objects may become the means of man's direct embrace by God's glory.

78. Can any man be so blind as not to see why, in light of all this, our Holy Fathers have expended such effort to ensure that anything which might diminish man's access to this sanctifying life is identified and cut away, and that what is handed down through the generations and comes to him is ever the approach to the one Church, identical to her actual nature? Every breath of her life presents man with the opportunity and means to be healed; therefore a right ecclesiology lies at the heart of each human creature's spiritual ascent.

79. The Fathers have fought to identify errors of belief, practice and comportment, not in order to be harsh or unduly rigid, but to preserve the salvific heart of their work. Every alteration of the Church's teachings represents a diminishment of the life of divine consolation and a wandering into the realm of sorrow and suffering. The Holy Fathers would protect us from such renewed grief, and have therefore dedicated themselves to providing the means to be prevented from it. The body of their

writings, and their practical guidance enshrined in the Holy Canons which the Spirit, through them, has bequeathed to the Church, represents precisely this.

80. The canonical order of the Church, which is these Fathers' legacy, together with the great host of their other writings and labors, must not therefore be considered as a "legal code" or merely a set of ancient regulations. It is the means by which the Fathers, inspired by the Holy Spirit, ensure that man is not led toward the darkness rather than the light.

81. These Holy Canons, too often denigrated by modern man's pharisaical and legalistic ideologies, are in fact one of the Church's most essential, loving gifts aimed precisely at the ascent into Godliness. Each Canon is a gift of sacred compassion: the evidence of the Truth, and the direction Truth provides through the dark maze of a world marred by sin.

82. The Canons are the guideposts of the Church's response to the world's variability, not made so arbitrarily but by the inspiration and assent of the Spirit, Who guides the Fathers and the councils in their pastoral response to the needs of the world.

83. Each Canon is the fruit of experience and compassion—the experience of error and of truth (for the battles fought to produce them were often long and arduous, and the Church did not shy away from confronting directly the many-headed hydra of error), and the compassion of the Church's pastors who do not wish for the pain of error to be repeated perpetually.

84. He who rejects the Canons, as they are rightly understood by the Church and implemented by the conciliar determinations of her God-fearing pastors, led by that same Spirit, rejects the God

Who leads His Church; for if one considers the Canons merely as the works of men, one has already denied the Spirit's governing presence in the Church and the inspiration of the Fathers by that self-same Spirit.

85. No man, be he layman, priest, bishop or even patriarch, has the right to overturn or dismiss the Holy Canons. It is the conciliar Spiritual inspiration of the Church that articulates her canonical consciousness, and only as such—receiving inspiration from the Spirit, discerned and articulated by the whole corpus of the Church, and not by any one part of her—does she speak, and speak with authority. For it is God Who speaks in her. The Creator governs His Church, not the creature.

86. To be clear on this essential point: the pastoral discretion of our hierarchs does not permit their abandonment of canonical norms, but rather their therapeutic application of them. One who attempts to abandon or contravene their spirit does not heal, but harms.

87. Amongst the many deficiencies in the Christian life in these latter days, a place of profound significance must be given to the general loss of a canonical consciousness. Too often a dismissiveness toward canonical order reigns. The axiomatic statement that "a Canon is a guide, not a law" is indeed true; but if this is raised as a means to evade the guidance the Canons give, in order to follow a path different from that they articulate, then even their role as guides is rejected.

88. It is our charge to live in gratitude and humility before the canonical guidance of the Church, and to permit it to shape our thinking and understanding; for it is a well fought-for inheritance

we have received from holy hierarchs, martyrs, pastors, and illumined teachers. This inheritance brings right ordering to our spiritual lives, but only if we will be guided by it, rather than seek to re-fashion it according to our fallen desires.

89. All the Canons in the world cannot direct aright the life of one who ignores them, or sets his own determinations above them. Those, however, who are prepared to submit their wills and intellects to those of the saints, will find in the Church's canonical governance the endless expression of God's care for each of His children. It will provide the means to avoid pitfalls, and to address the injuries caused by the falls we fail to avoid. It will provide chastisement to our laxity and solace to our weakness. It will rush to our aid in our brokenness, and ever lift us up into that which is greater than our present experience.

90. This does not mean that every Christian needs to be an expert in the Canons themselves; indeed, many fall into the dual traps of pride and judgment by attempting so to become without a blessing and without due guidance. The majority of the Holy Canons are intended principally for the scrutiny and adherence of the clergy, so that their ministry may be ordered aright and thus faithfully deliver the gift of salvation to the faithful. But it does mean that each Christian must understand that the Church is not orderless and chaotic, nor is she governed by whim or by private interpretation. She has a path marked out for her by God Himself, a shape contoured by the Creator.

91. A canonical consciousness is thus one in which the Christian lives in the awareness of that divine order that both establishes the Church and by which she in turn establishes our spiritual and liturgical lives. When we understand that the Church lives only

and ever after the pattern given her by the Spirit, and that we must conform the shape of our own lives to that pattern and be instructed by its precepts, then we have within us the glimmers of a canonical consciousness, even if we may be rarely called to read the Canons themselves.

92. Conversely, one who reads the Canons thoroughly and combs through them to their smallest phrase, yet does so in a manner of worldly legalism that seeks loopholes and exclusions, attempting manners of interpretation that patently aim to bend living tradition to a personal interpretation or prevalent ideology, does not possess the consciousness of the Church's canonical life at all.

93. Above all, what is required of each one of us is humility before the mind of the Church, and that a constant battle be waged against the demon of pride that would cause us to believe that our thoughts can be the interpreters of her Truth, rather than her Truth the only guide a director of our minds.

94. If and when we at last thus humble ourselves, we may arrive at the blessed state of illumination in authentic ecclesial life, by which we rightly understand that every breath of her utterance, every act of her counsel and every steady hand of her direction is the Church's manifestation of God's pastoral love for His flock.

95. Behold the love of Christ in His Church! There is no dimension of our life, however seemingly small or insignificant, that is not subject to the loving care of the Holy Fathers. Each Canon, like each sacred homily and theological text they have produced, is a gift of that care. Each is a sign of the extent of God's love for us.

96. Ultimately, all the Holy Canons play their due part in the work of faithfully guiding us back to that central reality: that the Life in Christ is a Mystery, in which the Holy Mysteries draw us into the depth of God's Grace and become the fountains of sanctification that transform the entirety of man's life into a spiritual creation.

97. The Church, the harbor of these Mysteries, is herself a Mystery, for in her the creature is united to its Creator and discovers in this world a communion in the Kingdom and a foretaste of true and eternal life.

98. The pursuit of Godliness is thus nowhere brought into the fullness of its potential, other than here. The Church is where Godliness abides, because it is the Church that makes men Godly. She is Holy, and so grants to humanity the abundance of her holiness, that she may with full confidence proclaim in the midst of God's sanctified creatures, "The holy things are for the holy!"[101]

99. And what greater or more wonderful mystery might there be, than that the human creature, fashioned so beautifully yet having stained himself so thoroughly with the blot of sin, might once again be made worthy of that word, "holy," in the eyes of God his Maker?

100. Glory to God Who comes to us in so wonderful a manner, rendering the earthly man spiritual and the broken man whole through the union in Himself that begins in this world, in time, and abides unto eternity.

V

A Century on Worship and Prayer, and the Ascent of Humanity to God

1. Upon this earth the Creator has bestowed the possibility of the vision of heaven; and more than the vision alone: the very participation in heavenly worship by the creature of dust and breath. The heavens have been revealed to man, and the earth has been made the Lord's tool to lead the creature into the embrace of the will of his God.

2. This is where true worship will lead you, Christian: to the very heights of Paradise. Think no less of this gift than to see it for what it is: a miracle, and a thing truly divine! God makes ready for man the ascent to the perfect heights of communion with Himself and the mystical entrance into His Kingdom.

3. Therefore that which stands at the beginning of man's spiritual ascent, the Kingdom of God and a renewed perception of it in man's life, stands also at its heights. The creature is called to partake directly of that divine reality he has long set before his eyes.

4. Indeed, eternal and perfect worship is the characteristic of the Kingdom of God—of His divine realm and manifest presence.

Its bestowal upon the created realm, the very world in which we sojourn, is no less than the gift of this Eternal God to those He has fashioned for that eternity, bestowed in order that they might partake, already in this present life, of that which defines the life to come.

5. Worship is thus the fruit of divine revelation, not human creation. Its origin is in heaven. Let every Christian heart understand this. Worshiping aright, man drinks on earth of waters that have been poured from eternity by God Himself, from the wellspring of His own Life—for "every good gift and every perfect gift is from above, and comes down from the Father of lights" (Jas 1:17), and the heavenly worship given to humankind is indeed a gift most perfect and sacred.

6. Moreover, the impetus for this sacred worship itself has its origin in the divine. It is not the human handiwork's desire to know God or reverence Him that leads to the advent of true worship; it is, rather, the fruit of the Lord's own desire to be known, and to make Himself accessible to His creation. God longs to be known by us even more than we long to know Him.

7. It is for this very reason that man was fashioned: that he might be the recipient of God's abiding love. As it is the nature of the Divine Persons of the Holy Trinity to exist in the perpetual, eternal embrace of co-inhering love, so the creature fashioned in the image of this Trinity is created in order to "abide in" the same "love" (cf. John 15:10; 1 John 4:16)—the love shared by and of God Himself.

8. Secular man believes that human need leads to humanity's creation of a deity, and the worship of it, to satisfy his ignorance

and fear; but the Christian knows that God pre-exists all and bestows true worship out of His abundance of love, before man even knows to yearn for it. Here we have a beautiful corrective for one of the presumptuous errors of modern man's struggling intellect. Whereas secular analysis perennially seeks to explain worship and even religion itself as a constructed response to humanity's longing to perceive something beyond itself, the reality is that the worshiping creature is fulfilling not its own desire, but its Creator's.

9. This worship, by which the Lord expresses His desire to be known, in turn unites man to the life of his Maker, conforming his heart to perfect adoration, his soul to perfect thanksgiving, and his life to unending joy in the God Who fashioned him. In this the Will of God is manifest; and in responding to this gift, it becomes our own longing as well.

10. In this, we may say rightly that God's revelation of the worship that draws man to Himself is the crown of His love for humanity. Through it, the gift of love is made whole: man's will comes to resemble the will of his Maker. If he embraces it, and by it is drawn into the divine, it fulfills also the purpose of his creation—to live in the joy of divine communion.

11. To put this another way, worship is the making complete of the human creature. When the Lord breathed into Adam's frame His own breath, "man became a living soul" (Gen 2:7); but it is only when Adam breathes that breath fully, when he inhales the life of God and responds to the calling to be united to Christ, "joined to the Lord" (1 Cor 6:17), that the living being becomes at last a true person.

12. Human personhood is defined by precisely this: the individual's coming to live in union with Christ, through Him being drawn into the life of the Holy Trinity. The ascent of holiness is one and the same with the ascent into true personhood. To be a person, as distinct from an individual, is not the automatic state of man—at least, not of man bound in the chains of sin. All are individuals, and precious as such; but personhood comes as the fruit of ascesis and sanctification.

13. Humanity is precious by its creation, sacred and holy as a handiwork beloved by its Maker. But a person is more than the handiwork: the human individual becomes a full person only in active communion with the Grace of God. Just as the Divine Persons of the Trinity exist ever and only in the communion they have with one another, so man becomes a person, fully manifesting the Image he bears, only when he attains communion with his Creator. This relation comes to describe his very being, too.

14. To put this another way: animate humanity exists in the creature being the handiwork of God; personhood resides in the handiwork's communion, through the Holy Spirit, in the Person of the Son of the Father. The one is already a good; the other is infinitely greater, and a thing truly divine.

15. Thus, worshiping aright, man finds the substance of himself. Here, at last, he is more than merely dust. Here the dust comes to breathe anew divine breath and be imbued with divine Life, for the gift of true worship is nothing less than communion in God Himself.

16. The ongoing work of man's creation is thus taken up anew in his worshiping life. The handiwork is held in the hands of the

Artist Who fashioned it—Who, through this means, wipes away the dirt of creation's abandonment and renews man's formation in sanctity.

17. Man is not rent from himself in this act, by no means! Rather, he finds the revelation of his true and abiding life, which has always been his communion with God. By worship turning him more fully toward his Fashioner, he draws closer to the fulfillment of his personal identity and discovers what is true in himself.

18. The apostasy of modern individualism falsely suspects faith and the veneration of God to involve a denial of self. Contemporary man fears that in worshiping God after a plan other than his own, he may "lose himself;" but it is precisely in the right worship of God that a man discovers, rather than loses, his authentic identity.

19. Apart from its life in God, the self is in fact little more than an idol, for it becomes a thing cherished—indeed almost worshiped—in place of the Lord rather than in gratitude toward Him. The "realization" of such a self can only be considered a delusion.

20. If you wish to be free, and in your freedom to be truly yourself, then worship the living God aright. So doing, you will find yourself liberated from the binding slavery of ingratitude and isolation, and the false dimensions of a feebly fabricated "life." You will, indeed, discover yourself anew, and aright; for the slave, being set free, finds a newness of life and the birth of a real identity.

21. Moreover, in responding to God's love with love, man discovers his own glory and highest joy. This being known to the Creator, Who knows all things, He created man to worship as much as to breathe; for the desire of the Fount of joy is the

attainment of joy by His creation, which brings glory to Himself and to the creature alike.

22. It is thus that the Lord reveals the modes and manners of sacred worship, leaving these not to man's ingenuity or will, for God Himself seeks by His own hand to establish His creation in what is right and good. Therefore He bestows right worship as a revelation of eternal truth, which might become man's internal inheritance; for it is not an external attribution of human life but an essential element of man's created being.

23. The human creature is fashioned to worship God not as an obligation or chore imposed upon his self-sustained existence, but an intrinsic dimension of the creative handiwork of the Author of Life. Right worship is a constituent element of a truly living human being.

24. Let the one who wishes to understand the nature of true worship, therefore, seek to behold the wisdom of the Creator. All creation is His direct and immediate work; it is not the fruit of accident, chance, or external design. God creates each "after its kind" (cf. Gen 1:11–12, 21, 24), to fulfill its purpose according to His intention. Thus it is, too, with each element of man's formation from the dust—the very creature that will find its fulfillment in divine worship. The One Who makes the dust and forms man from it, fashions his every sinew, each hair, the soul and his every interior facet.

25. Each element in this design, moreover, is intentional to the artistry of man's created glory. Each bone and organ and tissue has purpose, as does each attribute of the soul, the nous, the heart and all man's spiritual faculties. The living man is the concourse

of all these, designed and fashioned and received from God, in whom each element of his creation fulfills its part in the establishment of his full life. Adam is not left to "design" or "define" his flesh, nor bones, nor heart nor eyes; the Creator's Hands themselves fashioned these as is meet.

26. Neither is there arbitrariness or accident to the course of this living being's existence; nor are the paths of history left to man's design, despite his attempts to control and even thwart that history. The Law of Life is not composed but revealed (cf. Exod 20); the provision of the means of repentance is not devised but handed down to mankind from above[102]; and the coming of a longed-for salvation is likewise not the handiwork of humanity but of God Himself (cf. Gal 4:4–5). Both in his composition and his history, therefore, man's lot is consistent: the decisive elements are the fruit not of his own fashioning, but are the continuing creative labor of the Artificer of all things.

27. It is by living truthfully according to the nature of his fashioning, and following eagerly the revelation of the Way of Life, that Adam finds himself and walks toward God. To depart from that inheritance is to err, and ultimately to fall; to embrace it is ever to grow into perfection.

28. So, too, with the revelation of sacred worship. By it man breathes divine life and ascends toward the pinnacle of his created state: but this aspect of his existence is no more of his design or fashioning than any other. It, too, must be received. When man enters into the temple of God's glory, the fullness of his life at last begins; yet the creature, here as elsewhere, cannot rightly fashion that which can only come from the Creator. The

temple is life- and glory-bearing because it is God's and bestows communion with Him.

29. That which has its origin in man cannot bring to man what is beyond himself, but only more of himself. But that which is received from God may bestow every manner of divine blessing and Grace.

30. Testimony to this reality is borne across history. Every attempt to create the means of approaching God, rather than receive it, fails. Adam and Eve sought their own means of knowing God more deeply, and fell (cf. Gen 3:6–7). The people of Senaar sought their own means to ascend to God, and fell (cf. Gen 11:1–9). Saul, bearing even the dignity of an anointed king, sought his own method of bringing sacrifice to God, and was brought down (cf. 1 Kgdms 13:8–14). The lesson of these examples is not difficult to learn, if only we will heed them!

31. This goes beyond merely the structures and rites of worship: fallen man seeks ever more dramatically to claim for himself the dignity of God and His creative authority, constantly striving to replace Him with the fruit of his intellect and designs. We see this in our modern day in his desire to alter biology, to change the foundations of life, and so forth. Broken man strives always to become the Creator, rather than adore Him. Thus it comes as no great surprise that fallen man also strives to alter the sacred nature of true worship, to make it a thing of his own devising rather than that handed down by God, since adoration requires obedience rather than self-rule.

32. Let modern man's approach to the temple of his flesh serve as a useful ensign of his approach to the temples ordained by God for

His worship. When man is no longer content with the flesh God has given him, when he seeks constantly to alter it, "better" it, make it more an image of his own desire rather than that bestowed in love by another, it cannot startle us that he would also find fault with the temples of prayer God has fashioned, or the devotion He has prescribed to take place therein, all for the purpose of elevating this same man's life.

33. Man's so-called social consciousness is a marker of his spiritual state. The more he desires to be his own god and fashion all he surveys after the image of his own design, the less he will find solace and comfort in his approach to the only God Who really is—precisely because God truly exists; He is not a manufacture of social or personal intention.

34. Thus these two realities are interconnected: As man departs from God, he departs from himself; and as he departs from himself, he draws yet further away from God. An individual in the process of dehumanizing self-idolization is already ensnared deeply in the process of abandoning the Lord.

35. But it is the abandonment of God, and God's will, that in fact precedes man's abandonment of himself. It is after Adam betrays the Lord that he loses the purity of his self-perception, not before (cf. Gen 3:7–12).

36. Similarly, the abandonment of true worship in the right faith has preceded man's rejection of other foundational elements of his existence: a true perception of human nature, the sanctity of creation, and so on. Human rebelliousness, so nakedly prevalent especially in our latter days, had baulked at God's revelation of

worship and faith long before it began to baulk at God's design of the human creature, or the cosmos.

37. We are truly foolish if we cannot see the connection between these things! Worship reveals to man the destiny of his creation, the ultimate purpose of his life—and more than reveals it, actually enables it. When this is altered or abandoned, it follows only too predictably that his understanding of these very things will also be altered.

38. He who does not worship as God instructs and designs him to worship, cannot see himself as God sees him and fashioned him. He who does not see himself as God sees him, does not yet see himself at all.

39. Worse still, he who does not worship as God reveals to him the pattern of worship, cannot have his eyes opened, through that dimension of his created being, to the destiny of his life or the beauty of his sacred identity. He is like a blind man, rejecting the gift of sight.

40. Or, the one who determines to craft worship after his own designs is like a man given a telescope by a gifted astronomer, perfectly crafted to see into the vastness of the heavens with clarity of vision, but who determines that he would prefer its lens to be bent another way, or its glass to be made of some more fashionable color. What does he gain as a result of these self-determined designs? That which looks like a telescope, and at first had its origin as the same, but which now sees only the vaguest outline of what once was clearly perceived.

41. So it is with the many and varied modern attempts to craft a worship of the living God that is other than that which He Himself

bestowed upon His precious Orthodox Church. They may bear similarities to true Christian worship, they may even maintain elements of a shared history, when traced back through the annals of the centuries; but each departure from and variation of that which was revealed by God is ultimately a disfiguration that diminishes this reality amongst those who, by it, embrace something less than the whole.

42. So, too, each rejection of the continuing revelation of that worship that resides in the hands of the ever-active Spirit Who guides the Church. Worship is a living reality, and its shape manifests God's response to man's need. Once He instructed rocks be lain atop each other (cf. Exod 20:25; Deut 27:5–6); later He commanded a sanctuary, then a Temple (cf. Exod 29:43–45; 33:9–11; 3 Kgdms 8:10–13); and so through history He continues to shape our experience of worship according to precisely what He determines is most needed by us, to draw us close to the eternal worship of heaven.

43. "Liturgical archaeology," as it is sometimes characterized— that is, the attempt to justify changes to the Church's living practice by reference to a custom that prevailed in the past—is as much as rejection of the Spirit's actual and ongoing governance of the Church as it is a means of projecting man's current desires onto the shape of worship, using glimmers of the past to justify his designs on the present.

44. He, by contrast, who receives true worship as a gift fashioned by God and not by his own hands, accepting what has been given as the perfect craftsmanship of the Artificer of all, is one who—if we may continue with our analogy of the telescope— receives not only the perfect tool to behold the clarity of the stars,

but a tool crafted to that end by none other than the Fashioner of the stars themselves. God-revealed worship is the tool of the Craftsman for the beholding of His craft. And more than this, for the participation in His craft; for God fashioned the cosmos not merely to be observed, but to be the very source of growth into eternity. As God has made every element of creation with precision and for a purpose, so each element of sacred worship, as it has been revealed to mankind, is precise and intentional in its manifestation.

45. The intention of this divine worship is not chiefly to be understood, and thus feed the intellect, but to inundate the creature with the experience of Grace and thus transform the soul. It does not so much teach man about creation and eternity as draw him into the immediate experience of both.

46. Worship may be pedagogical, yes; but it is above all experiential. In worship, man learns through his doing.

47. Moreover, worship is both man's doing (i.e., a work he undertakes, actions in which he engages), but also the avenue for what is done to him—that which acts upon him. This is why we call true worship *divine*: for not only is the human creature active in its movements, but so too is God Himself.

48. The temple is the God-appointed meeting place of heaven and earth and the locus of this divine–human encounter. It is the mountaintop upon which the face of God may be beheld (cf. Exod 33:11); the dark cloud of the Lord's sacred revelation, into which Moses entered at the peak of Mount Sinai (cf. Exod 19:3, 9, 16, 20); the haven of luminous darkness,[103] which makes bright the face of man through the uncreated illumination of

God's very presence; the mount of Tabor upon which uncreated Glory is beheld by the creature (cf. Matt 17:1–8, Mark 9:2–8, Luke 9:28–36).[104]

49. In the temple, man touches upon the deepest mysteries of life. That which is "hidden from eternity, a mystery unknown even to the angels," is made manifest in his presence.[105] That which is beyond eternity is brought to him in time. The infinite is brought close and made accessible to the touch of his lips.

50. Not only the mysteries that take place within it, but also the very structure of the temple, ordained by God, brings to the access of man's senses that which his mind cannot fully comprehend. The space representing heaven[106] touches the space representing earth,[107] divided by the wall of man's sin—the doors of the Creator's triumph over such sin opened in the presence of the sinner himself.[108] The shape of this sacred space, which has come down to us from our ancestors, to whom it was revealed directly by God, is itself a revelation of human history and God's presence.[109]

51. It is not only the Temple's physical structure that is revelatory, but also that which takes place within it, and even the person and attire of those who enact its sacred services. Within the temple the Priest is clothed as Christ, and we behold in him, as in an icon, the miracle of man's redemption.[110] Adam finds his fulfillment and perfection as he, the first man—represented in the black undergarments of the Priest—is clothed with the Grace of Christ. Over the black is lain gold and silver and the various colors of our liturgical life, demonstrating for us, each time the Priest stands in his sacred vesture, the possibility of Adam's redemption: of the old man becoming new, "clothed in

the garments of salvation" (cf. Isa 61:10), adorned in "honor and majesty" (cf. Job 40:10) and finding his sanctification in the Spirit.

52. At times, therefore, the Priest represents Adam to us, at times Christ—but is the self-same individual who is seen as both. And it is precisely as these two images *collide* in his person, in the movements of the sacred offices, that we perceive the reality of our redemption most clearly: the living and sacred icon of the First Adam becoming the New Adam, and humanity finding its truest identity in Christ.

53. Let us provide one poignant example of this living iconography of our worship: At the beginning of the evening service of Great Vespers, the Priest most clearly represents Adam, naked and bereft of formal attire, standing only in his black robes, save for the epitrahil and cuffs that are the ever-present signs of the dignity of his priesthood.[111] The Priest exits the Holy Altar and stands upon the solea facing toward the Altar, face to face with the Royal Doors which are closed before him, a visual reminder of Adam looking back into Paradise, as if through its closed gates, toward all that had been lost in his rebellion (cf. Gen 3:24), whilst the choir sings the great Psalm of creation, "Bless the Lord, O my soul…" (Ps 103), recounting the wonders of the world God has fashioned, from which Adam has alienated himself. In his dress, in his position before the closed doors, accompanied by the words of the Psalm, we encounter a vivid experience of the history of creation, sin, and our alienation from our Maker.

54. Yet the next time that the Priest appears in the same Divine Service, he is arrayed in fuller vestments, radiant. As the choir sings of the "Gentle Light" that comes into the world,[112] the Priest arrives, now arrayed as Christ, accompanied by either a candle

or the Gospel book (representing the Light that comes into the world, and the Gospel of salvation), and the Royal Doors are opened. What had been barred to Adam is opened by Christ! Heaven and earth, separated by sin, are united in the incarnation. Here, in visual representation, is the great message of hope summed up in the ancient words of St Cyril: "Adam, God's first-formed man, transgressed: could God not at once have brought death upon him? But see what the Lord does, in His great love toward man: He casts him out from Paradise, for because of sin he was unworthy to live there; but He puts him to dwell over against Paradise: that seeing whence he had fallen, and from what and into what a state he was brought down, he might afterwards be saved by repentance."[113] This is precisely what we behold: the New Adam steps out of eternity into creation, and draws creation into the Kingdom—and all this is symbolized in the dress and movements of the clergy within the temple.

55. The structure, and even the very presence in the world of the temple, put flesh and bone to our ascent into God's holiness. The temple stands amidst the other structures of the world as a signal of God's presence in creation, and His redemption of it—thus we strive to make our churches beautiful and visibly distinct from the architecture around them wherever this is a possibility. The temple stands in the midst of creation as a sign of holiness and the fact of God's immediate presence.

56. When we enter into this sacred space, there is manifested in us, by this very entry, the whole spiritual ascent of man. We seek to depart from our debasement, our weakness, arriving into the embrace of the strength and glory of the eternal God. Thus the temple has a narthex, a porch, symbolizing our passage from

the snares of this life into the presence of the Redeemer of life. Similarly, we do not simply walk into the temple as we might do any other building, without thinking. We pause before the doors, cross ourselves, say a prayer—aware that even the 'simple' act of entering the sacred space is a moment of participation in a mystery beyond this world.

57. But what of the world outside? Is not the world itself, the creation of God's own hands, already holy and sacred in its own right? Such a question is often raised by those who doubt the need for a specific structure or locus of sanctity, as if the holiness of all creation renders a specific temple unnecessary. The true Christian would banish this false dichotomy before giving it any attention; yet for the sake of weakness let us offer clarity. Of course creation is, by its nature, sacred: it is the handiwork of God Who creates naught but what is good and holy. And though this creation bears the mark of man's transgressions (cf. Gen 3:17–19), being weighed down by our iniquities and sins into a state in which "the whole creation groans and labors" in pain (Rom 8:22), the earth remains God's handiwork, and therefore, in its own right, the agent of His glory. Yet this is in no way discordant with the reality of a special element of creation by which the rest is sanctified and lifted up. This is a fact to which witness is borne by none other than God Himself: He Who created the cosmos Himself ordered worship to take place within it. He who fashioned the stones, blessed stones to be raised to His glory, as we have already stated (see again Exod 20:25; Deut 27:5–6). He Who "art everywhere present and fillest all things"[114] sent His Presence uniquely into the Ark, and the Sanctuary, and the Temple.[115] He Who is served by all He created, even the angels

themselves, instructed man to serve and worship in a unique way, after a unique manner, in a unique place.

58. Should we say therefore that God was ignorant of the fact of His presence in all places, when He ordered the construction of a Sanctuary for the reverence of His glory, instructing that men "shall make me a Sanctuary, and I will appear among [them]" (Exod 25:8)? or that all creation gives Him praise, when He instructed that specific praise should be offered in a precise manner?[116] Such a thought is ridiculous. Rather, it has always been God's will that in the grand temple of creation as a whole, specific locales should be sanctified, dedicated to the experience of His presence.

59. The Christian temple is itself made from creation, the fruit of man's artistry with the substance thereof, at God's command. It is made of stone and wood and paint and glass, all of which are drawn from the fabric of the earth that God has fashioned. So assembled and ordained by His command, they become instruments of a profound and pronounced sanctity within the broad harbor of creation.

60. When considered aright, this is no more unusual than the admission that in a loving relationship between, for example, a mother and child, there cannot be moments, places and encounters of distinct love, which bring the love that exists more generally into immediate and direct experience. When a mother embraces her child, in that singular, physical encounter, a world of love and affection, tenderness and sacrifice, is made real. Does that love, or sacrifice, not exist apart from that embrace? To think it does not would be absurd. Rather, in that embrace, the love

that exists is strengthened, assured, and renewed. Entering into the temple, we likewise transcend our day-to-day experience of this life, passing into an experience of focus upon the sanctity that ought to be perceived at all times.

61. The Christian, entering the temple, passes from the exterior world of the disordered and unfocussed senses, through the porch (which we have mentioned before), and into the Nave, a place of holiness, which in older times was referred to as "the holy place" (cf. Exod 26:33), and further represents now the great hull of the ship of salvation that guides us into eternity.[117] Within this holy space, his senses are focused and aimed toward yet greater heights, as the Christian looks toward the east, to the rising of the Sun, the birthing-place of life, and beholds—still at some distance and yet far closer to hand than before—the realm of Paradise: the sanctuary of heaven, brought here so very near to his presence.

62. Behold, in this sacred space, we are lifted up to the Kingdom, even as we witness the heavens crouching low to touch us. The Christian who stands in the temple, and communes therein, is at one and the same time on earth and in heaven.

63. In order fully to experience this reality, as God intends it, we must guard it and preserve it, as delivered by God through His saints. It is a source of sorrow when we behold, in some places, the modification of the sacred worship of the Church, based on revisionist conceptions of religion and faith. Every generation produces some who believe they know, better than God, what is best-suited to the salvation of His children; and thus every generation produces those who would re-fashioned what God has

delivered, in order to make it more "palatable" or "accessible" to the proclivities of contemporary man.

64. Amongst the most common, in our own day, are those who seek to alter the shape of the temple itself, or at least the usage of the traditional elements within it—and most especially, the iconostasis and the doors thereof. In not a few places one can find temples where the Royal Doors are always open; or where the iconostasis itself is reduced almost to nonexistence, so that what is beyond is always visible in its entirety to those in the Nave; or where elements appointed to take place outside the Altar instead happen within, or vice-versa. These, I must say, are deeply sorrowful losses of the means of a sacred experience. They are most often the fruits of an intellectualization of worship: of reducing it to a pedagogical lesson in which one cannot understand what he cannot hear, or benefit from what he does not see. But as we have had occasion to say more than once before, some knowledge comes from a different kind of experience and action—and this has been, since the first moments of its revelation, the normal character of Christian worship.

65. Let us take, as an example, the experience brought to man through the presence of the iconostasis in the temple, and the opening and closing of its doors. As close as heaven has bent itself to us, as high as we may have climbed through the help of the saints and the Church herself, man must know that there stands always between us and God, between this life of my sinful flesh and the eternal life of the glorified body, a great "wall": a division, a separation, which is my transgression. This, through the great mercy that God offers in his Church, is made real for us in the experience

of spiritual ascent that every entrance into the temple represents, through the great wall of icons constructed between the Holy Place and the Most Holy—between our symbolic heaven and earth. That wall, that barrier, is not merely an idea: it is manifest to us in full profundity as a physical reality, walling off our immediate experience from that of yet greater and holier things.

66. This, too, is something that has been part of God's instruction for man's worship since the first. The divinely commanded structure of the earlier Sanctuary and Temple included a great veil, a barrier separating the Holy Place from the Holy of Holies (cf. Exod 26:31–33; 35:11; 2 Chr 3:14). God has always drawn close to man, and sought to bring man close to Himself; but He has always done this through the accentuation of the reality of sin, so that the creature knows its true place before his God. It is precisely through this awareness that the real intimacy of the overcoming of sin can be fully attained; for "the Lord Jesus had compassion upon us in order to call us unto Himself, not frighten us away."[118]

67. This is a gift of the Spirit's ongoing inspiration of the Church, a proof of the guidance of God: that while, in the first days of our ecclesial life, when the Church was in worldly terms young upon the earth, wandering from village to village, worshiping in synagogues and homes, it did not have this physical barrier that had long been part of its worshiping life in the Temple; yet the Spirit so guided God's flock in understanding and wisdom that this, too, would be gradually introduced into the architecture of our holy temples, in order that the symbolism which touches the heart would not be lost, but increased through the guidance of the Most Holy Spirit.

68. Yet, some protest, was not the veil of the temple *torn in two* upon the crucifixion of the most-merciful Saviour of the world (cf. Matt 27:51)? Was not the glorious resurrection of the Lord sufficient to tear apart that which had served to barricade man from his God? Alas, would we only have eyes truly to see, rather than impose our limited understanding upon spiritual realities too wonderful for us, that are of heights we cannot attain (cf. Ps 138:6 LXX)! Yes, in truth, as the Lord offered up His soul upon the Cross, dying a true death in order to arise in true Life, the ancient veil sewn by His most-pure Mother was rent asunder. Yet its meaning was not lost, nor its symbolism dissolved, in that miraculous act of testimony. It is precisely in the rending apart of the veil that we come to understand the nature of our redemption in God. If there is no veil to be torn asunder, we struggle to understand both the nature of the barrier our sin poses to a holy life and the nature of Christ's redeeming us from it. The rending apart of the veil in Herod's Temple upon the mount was an historical reality that took place in one moment, in one period of history—a sacred piece of the story of our redemption. And yet, we are deluded if we believe that the veil constructed by our own sin, the barrier that I erect between my own life and God's unerring holiness, does not yet exist, and persist—as if it were somehow banished already in some other age.

69. My sin poses a barrier to holiness every time I succumb to it: every time I indulge the passions, or wander from the arms of my Redeemer. This barrier, this veil, also must be rent in twain, not once but continually, that my sin not divide me forever from my God. And thus it is in our sacred temples: the iconostasis is this veil, this wall and barrier, constructed precisely so that,

liturgically, we might tear it down. In each Divine Service, where so appointed, that *tearing asunder* is symbolized by the opening of the doors, allowing that which is *in heaven* freely to pass to that which is *on earth*; and that which is on earth to gain access to that which is in heaven. When the doors of the iconostasis, rightly closed at all appointed times, are then opened at the prescribed moments, we see—and, iconographically, participate in—the tearing apart of the veil that lies within each of us, in the temple of our hearts.

70. The presence of this iconostasis does not fill us with fear or despair, but with longing—for we see upon it the Apostles, the prophets, the patriarchs, the angels, and the saints of generation upon generation who have pointed us toward the overcoming of our sin. Their presence creates a yearning, arising from the vision of their faces before and amongst us, and together with them we strive to receive the Grace of Christ that may destroy the veil of sin within the temples of our lives.

71. How much is thus torn away from man, when these things are removed from his experience of worship by those who, through revisionist pride, would make it more "accessible" by diminishing an iconostasis to a mere railing, or designing it in such a way that it can easily be seen over, or through, "so that it does not divide"; or who abandon the symbolically rich opening and closing of the doors so that the faithful "do not feel cut off" from what happens beyond them. They very thing they need most to feel, they cannot! Worse, they cannot experience the liturgical transformation of that experience: the power of that separation's symbolic "destruction," right in their midst.

72. The above is but a singular example of the necessity to treat as a sacred inheritance, and so to preserve, the whole of the revelation of worship that the Church provides for us, and not modify it according to our whims. Our understanding is so often fragmentary, impulsive; but the Church guides us into something greater—into the experience, through our worshiping life, of an encounter with God that is not only historical, in that it has been revealed throughout history by the Lord of history, but also deeply personal and ever-present, in that it takes place in, with and for the individual human person, always in the present moment of his or her lived experience.

73. It is necessary for the Christian to live in the experience of God, as He provides it, which can only take place in the present. The past is already dead, the future we anticipate may not be given to us; it is only today that the Life in Christ is lived. The more that we cling to what has gone before, or live in the self-crafted expectation of what might come tomorrow, the less we respond to the face of Christ that confronts us today.

74. This Christ, the second Person of the Holy Trinity, Son of the Father, has entered into history uniquely. He walked upon the earth in a certain place, at a definite moment, in the presence of particular others. These things were concrete; prior to them the world waited in expectation, after them it recollects this sacred history. Yet the One Who came into history is the pre-eternal God beyond the bounds of time, Who exists within and also apart from history, Who was yesterday and will be tomorrow, but always *is* today—the One Who ever exists, as is said in the Divine

Services[119]; the "Alpha and Omega" experienced now, as He says of Himself (cf. Rev 22:13).

75. The experience of this God is always a uniquely present experience. We worship the One Who "was"—that is, Who was with all generations before us—and we say repeatedly of God that He is glorified "forever," even "unto the ages of ages, amen!"—that is, that He will be also with future ages. But we say this only after confessing each time that He is glorified *now*, experienced *now*, encountered *now*, and so forever. That is to say, we bless our God Who exists and Whom we encounter, as He always is, in this present moment: "Him who is and who was and who is to come" (Rev 1:4).

76. The hymns of the Church remind us of this with careful attentiveness. *Today* Christ is born in Bethlehem, they proclaim. *Today* salvation is come into the world. *Today* death is trampled down. There is, of course, an historical "before" and "after"; yet we do not live in those historical categories—we live only today. Today is "the day which the Lord hath made" (Ps 117:24 LXX); "now is the day of salvation" (2 Cor 6:2).

77. It is this moment, and this moment alone, that is the sanctified and grace-filled arena in which I may fight the spiritual fight that leads to glorification.

78. This reality is not only present in the language of our liturgical experience; it is meant to be the reality that shapes how we approach and experience the whole of life, molded in its highest form by our liturgical encounter. Memory and intellect may operate in the past, but the immediate senses only operate in the present. Thus we are present where our senses lead us, and so the

Church leads us precisely through the senses to the present experience of Divine Grace.

79. Through the complete inundation of the whole creature in the Divine Services—sight, in the holy icons and sacred movements; hearing, in the chanting and singing; scent in the fragrant incense; movement, in the prostrations and signs of the precious Cross; and so on—we are continually brought out of memory and intellectualization, into the direct experience of that in which we are made participants.

80. The struggle to depart from the chains of the past is difficult for many; and this is precisely what a clinging to transgression and sorrow become: chains that bind us. The events of the past may hold so great a spell over a person that the memory of them becomes, in a strange way, his present. If, as is truly the case, the worship of God draws us ever more constantly into the immediate *presence* of God, it is the devil's desire, by contrast, to draw man ever more despondently into the *bondage* of his wrongs. The evil one seeks to bind us to the past, and to make us fear the future.

81. Those who succumb to such temptation live their lives, day to day, not in the full experience of God, or even of what is around them, but in the remembered experience of what has gone before or the fearfully anticipated experience of what may come. This is true with negative memories, but also positive ones. When such memory dictates our present experience, we must recognize that which has become passionate (i.e., made us passive), and which binds us not to life but to death.

82. Such chains can feel especially heavy with respect to one's past life, whether on account of some dramatic sin that continues

to loom over us interiorly, or perhaps many or even innumerable sins that seem to have been the very fabric of our earlier lives. Sometimes it is the sins of others, rather than only one's own, that plague a man's memory: evils done to him in his youth, or mistreatment by family or close ones. The continual recollection of such traumas (for not only is evil done against us a type of trauma, but our own sin is a trauma against the divine beauty in which God fashioned us) wraps these heavy chains more tightly around the heart, preventing it from moving forward or fully functioning even now.

83. It is precisely for such a reason that the worship God has delivered to us contains so many elements intended to draw us out of our passions and free us to experience God and be transformed by Him. We have seen this in the architecture, the movements, even the dress appointed for our worship—not to mention the sacred words delivered by God through the Scriptures and the saints. It is the same truth that is present, too, in the Mysteries of the Church themselves,[120] by which the Lord invites us into the immediate experience of His power and Grace, and each of which in its own way draws us out of the bondage of the passions and into the ever-present reality of God's love.

84. Amongst these Mysteries, that of the confession and absolution of our sins is absolutely essential to the ascent into holiness. We will never grow in spiritual freedom unless we free ourselves from the chains of our past through the Mystery of Confession, practiced with zeal and diligence as frequently as possible.

85. Confession is the cleansing of the heart by none other than the Maker of the heart. We identify it as a Mystery, a Sacrament, because it is not merely the recitation of man's sins by the sinner,

which would be a purely human work; nor is it solely the address of man's sins by the Priest, which would be little more than mere human counsel. Confession is a Sacrament because it is the offering of an open heart to God, Who in turn comes to cleanse, purify, fill and change that heart.

86. Confession is not some legal requirement gone through in order to obtain a writ of forgiveness for our wrongs from the Lord, Who in any case knows of and is merciful toward our sins even before we become aware of them; it is the transformation of our heart into the altar of our innermost temple, upon which we offer the broken reality of our soul—the only fruit we have to bear—and seek its transformation by the Lord into that which might be life-creating rather than death-bearing.

87. Within the Church temple, the Priest brings bread and wine and by God's Grace these become His very Body and Blood. Within our personal temple—our body and soul—the Priest helps us to bring our lives, beautiful in formation yet so sinful in actuality, and offer these at the altar of Confession, whereby the Lord may transform them also.

88. In this, a true miracle is enacted in a genuine confession. It is not a counseling session or analogue to secular therapy: it is God accepting the offering of a broken heart, and making it whole in return.

89. Yet even those who heartily confess the whole content of their lives might still feel the chains of their sinfulness binding them, and not sense the transformation wrought by God's own hands. They might dwell yet upon their transgressions, and then begin to despair: "How can I be so trapped by my past life, even when

I have laid bare all my sins in Confession? Can there be no hope of escape from what has gone before?" Let there be a few words of counsel for these moments of doubt. Remember first of all that sins, truly confessed and absolved, are genuinely forgiven. This basic, yet miraculous, fact of Christian life is one that the broken heart sometimes struggles to believe. "I will believe in the resurrection, in the virgin birth, in the healing of the sick and the giving of sight to the blind; but I cannot truly believe that God forgives me, so freely, of the wrongs I have done!" But belief in the forgiveness offered by the Lord is precisely a matter of faith: it goes so strongly against our experience in this fallen life that accepting the true nature of God's love becomes an element of belief that must be exercised, nurtured and practiced, just as all the others.

90. The heart does not change its disposition in an instant, when for so long we have shaped it awry. As we come to accept the reality of divine forgiveness we must understand at the same time that, even when a sin has been forgiven, it does not simply vanish from our memory. It can still have a negative effect upon our heart; it can still be permitted to affect us; we can still succumb to its reality, or the memory of it. But here is the essential fact: the sin that has been confessed and forgiven need no longer chain down our heart by an insufferable force that cannot be escaped.

91. Before Confession and absolution, the power of a sin over us is fierce, its presence within us no longer in our power to control or expel—for "the wages of sin is death" (Rom 6:23), and death is beyond our means to conquer. After Confession, however, that power is crushed by the Lord's heel, since the Sacrament of Confession is a direct encounter with the Grace of God, Who is stronger than our sins.

92. Through Confession, the heart is liberated from the enslaving grip of the sin we lay bare; the chains are broken—and yet, as we have said, we may still elect to hold onto those chains. This is what happens when we linger in the memory of the past: it is no longer the sin that holds its grip on us, but we who grip onto it, never letting it truly depart our interior life. Though the Lord has unbound the chains of our heart, we cling to them, and so we continue to suffer.

93. In the icon of the Defeat of Hades, we see symbolically depicted the broken chains of hell. We hear about this, too, in the hymns of Pascha—the season in which this icon is normally brought into the center of the temple, taken as the chief icon of the Resurrection. But of course, Hades itself has no literal chains; the power that keeps men there is not one of physical steel or iron barring a door. The chains that are destroyed in the Resurrection are those over our own hearts. It is there, in the heart, that sin and death were locks that could not be undone by man's own power; and it is there, in the heart, that Christ sets man free. Hades itself, which is a reality and not a myth or metaphor, is nevertheless nothing more than a place conformable to the suffering of the enslaved heart. Yet, how terrible is that unnecessary suffering!

94. To live in the present experience of God is to be willing to let go of the chains of past sin that the Lord has defeated and absolved. A man cannot live in the constant agony of his past, nor does God wish him to do so. God "called you out of darkness and into His marvelous light" (1 Pet 2:9); and just as light does not shine in the past, but in the present, this is precisely the place to which God draws us through every element of divine worship.

95. To worship the living God is to enter into the immediate presence of none other than this God. It is to set aside, for a moment, the affairs of this life, our "worldly cares,"[121] that God may change our hearts and enable us to transform every moment into one imbued with His love—a love capable of changing and redeeming the world.

96. Let him who seeks the Kingdom of God, therefore, seek it nowhere else than in the Life in Christ by which God draws us into that Kingdom as His own work and the fulfillment of His own desire. A Godly life consists in one's life being bound to God's; spiritual ascent must always be the approach to the Spirit. The Holy Trinity fashions us for this Life, and through the worship He reveals to us, provides us the artful, and most beautiful, means to attain it.

97. So, Christian, strive to attain what is attainable! Though we are weak, God may make us strong. Though we are sinful, God may render us pure. Though we are feeble, God may grant us strength. Take courage always in this: that it is the longing and will of the God of All that the whole of creation be perfected in you, and that you—the precious and utterly unique work of His hands—may add to the beauty of creation that irreplaceable element for which He fashioned you from the dust. All of creation sings to God, but He longs that it sing together with you, and you with it, in a chorus of praise that never ends.

98. Hear anew the words of the Apostle who, recounting the great examples of faith across generations and millennia, including the sacred saints and martyrs "of whom the world was not worthy" (Heb 11:38), reminds that their story is not complete

until it involves you, and each of us, who would turn to God in hope: for "all these, having obtained a good testimony through faith, did not receive the promise, God having provided something better for us, that they should not be made perfect apart from us" (Heb 11:39, 40).

99. God is with us! Let us, even if we are very late in setting about doing so, at last live in the knowledge of this gift, and offer our lives as a response to love to Him Who "first loved us" (1 John 4:19), and Who loves us still.

100. O Christ Who hast made the heavens and the earth, we are awed by Thy beauty! Thou hast adorned creation with splendor, the work of a master Artist, that our weak hearts might behold Thy beauty and so learn to be beautiful. Open our eyes, therefore, to see what Thou hast prepared for all mankind. Teach us to take delight in the great mountains and the little flowers, the glories of Thy temples and the tender fragility of our souls, that by Thy mercy we might join Thy saints and the whole of creation, crying out to Thee in unending song: to Thee be glory, now and unto the endless ages. Amen!

A CONCLUDING WORD

Whether, in the end, my attempt in this little book—to bring together some of the thoughts of the Holy Fathers on the pursuit of Godliness in this life—will prove useful to those who might read it, I do not know. I know only that my sole desire has been to share a little of what I, like countless other Orthodox Christians before me, have received from the Apostles and the Apostolic Church. In this age of darkness and apostasy, they have given me hope, and the assurance that God conquers all. In a generation of revisionism and self-created "truth," they have given me the steadfast assurance that God does not change, nor does His love, nor the Truth that only comes from Him and is found in Him. In the painful recognition of my own sinfulness and weakness, they have given me the immeasurable blessing of knowing a God Who sees the beauty in even the darkest soul, and Who longs for nothing more than to bring it into the light of redemption. And what we have been given, we are meant to share.

The world today is in so many ways difficult, especially for the Christian. So much of it has been given over to debased human passion, fear, and hatred. So much is grounded in the acceptance of the very things that in previous generations the human race would have more readily considered its enemies: self-will, self-definition, and boorish self-centeredness. It has too easily, and too dramatically, let go of its spiritual bearing and opted for sand and shadows to replace it; and so hope has drifted away, and man feels ever more lost, ever more alone—with seemingly nothing to do about it.

But the message of redemption is still there, still being proclaimed by those to whom God gives the courage and the strength to confess it. From them we, even today, might hear the same message of hope that came to Adam when he was cowering beneath the trees after his transgression, as the Lord sought him out to redeem him; and the same message of hope that came to the Apostles and the faithful women disciples who, weeping over the torture they had experienced at the Cross, were sought out by the risen Christ Who came to replace their tears with joy. It is the same message that gave strength to the martyrs as they found joy in making their sacrifice for their Lord; and it is the same message that inspires those whom the world is making into martyrs in our own day, suffering for our suffering Saviour and remaining unbending in their life in the Truth, whatever lies may be thrown at them. The Christian message has not changed. It will not change. Millennia after Christ first commissioned His Apostles to go forth into the world, we who unworthily follow them as Christians are still saying the same things.

And Christ is still seeking out mankind. He is the Truth that does not change, that does not falter, and He does not cease to provide to His children the path of spiritual ascent that leads to life with, and in, Himself. Though the devil may persistently whisper in our ears that there is no hope, no purpose to life, modern man must at last gain the resolve of his forebears and have the courage to reject this ancient lie. Godliness is obtainable: it is the free gift of the Lord. Pursuing it should be our aim, our happiness, our struggle, and our salvation.

May we all receive the strength for this pursuit from the Holy Church, which God has provided to lead us into life. And may we live that life without fear, without hesitation, that we might not only read about the saints and hear their testimony, but follow their example and—by the mercy of Him Who fashioned us as He fashioned them—join them in the eternity of the Kingdom of our Creator.

Amen!

NOTES

Throughout the present work, patristic quotations cited with reference to a modern edition are quoted in the translation of that edition; those without reference to a modern edition are the translations of the present author.

Introduction

1   E.g. in Bishop Irenei, "A Century on Prayer and Watchfulness" and "A Second Century on Prayer: On the Preparation of the Mind and Heart," in *The Beginnings of a Life of Prayer* (2012; second edn. 2017), pp. 70–117.

2   St Maximus the Confessor, "Foreword to Elpidios the Presbyter," prefacing his *Four Centuries on Love*, para. 1; translation in G. Palmer, P. Sherrard and K. Ware, *The Philokalia: The Complete Text*, vol. II (New York: Faber & Faber, 1981), p. 52.

Chapter 1

3   St Makarios the Great, *Fifty Spiritual Homilies*, 43.7 (Dorries, 289); trans. J.A. McGuckin, *Mystical Chapters: Meditations on the Soul's Ascent from the Desert Fathers and Other Early Christian Contemplatives* (Boston: Shambala Publications, 2002), Praktikos 83, p. 54.

4   See St Augustine of Hippo, *Confessions*, 1.1.1: "Thou hast made us for Thyself, and our hearts are restless until they rest in Thee."

5   Abba John of Apamea (John the Solitary), *Second Dialogue with Thomasios* (Lavenant, SC 311.61); trans. in *Mystical Chapters*, Praktikos 13, p. 21.

6   See St Athanasius the Great, *On the Incarnation of the Word,* 43.3: "Now, nothing in creation had gone astray with regard to its notions of God, save man alone. Neither sun, nor moon, nor heaven, nor the stars, nor water nor air swerved from their order; but knowing their Artificer and Sovereign, the Word, they remain as they were fashioned. But men alone, having rejected what was good, devised things of nought instead of the truth, and have ascribed the honour due to God, and their knowledge of Him, to demons and men in the shape of stones."

7   St Makarios the Great, *Fifty Spiritual Homilies*, 43.3 (Dorries, 286); in *Mystical Chapters*, Praktikos 14, pp. 22, 23.

8   St John Klimakos, *The Ladder of Paradise*, 19.8; trans. in *Mystical Chapters*, Praktikos 50, p. 41.

9   Employed as the introductory phrase to the Beatitudes that are most commonly appointed as the Third Antiphon of the Divine Liturgy. The phrase is inserted yet more often during the Great Fast when the Typica are used.

10   *Apophthegmata Patrum*, Joseph of Panephysis, 7; *The Sayings of the Desert Fathers*, p. 103; trans. in B. Ward, *The Sayings of the Desert Fathers: The Alphabetical Collection* (Kalamazoo: Cistercian Publications, 1975), p. 103.

11   St Maximus the Confessor, *Second Century on Love*, 59; in *The Philokalia*, vol. II, 75.

12   St Thalassios the Libyan, *Second Century on Love, Self Control and Life in Accordance with the Intellect*, 1; in *The Philokalia*, vol. II p. 313.

13   See St Mark the Ascetic, *On the Spiritual Law*, 100: "Avarice is clearly a product of these two components [self-esteem and sensual pleasure]"; cf. §99; in *The Philokalia*, vol. I,117.

14   Ibid., 104.

15   Abba John of Apamea, *Second Dialogue with Thomasios* (Lavenant, SC 311.61).

16   See the anonymous epistle *Ad Diognetum*, 6.1.

17   St Justin Popovich; trans. from quotation in Metropolitan Hierotheos (Vlachos) of Nafpaktos, *Orthodox Monasticism* (Birth of the Holy Theotokos Monastery, 2011), pp. 55, 56.

18   St Anthony the Great, Saying 1 in the *Apopthegmata* of the Desert Fathers, Thematic Collection, "Progress in Perfection"; trans. B. Ward, *The Desert Fathers: Sayings of the Early Christian Monks* (Penguin Classics, 2003).

19   St Arsenios, from the *Apopthegmata*, alphabetical collection, 3.

20   St Theodoros the Ascetic, *A Century of Spiritual Texts*, 100; in *The Philokalia*, vol. II, 37.

Chapter 2

21   Cf. St Thalassios the Libyan, *First Century on Love, Self Control and Life in Accordance with the Intellect*, 89; in *The Philokalia*, vol. II, p. 312.

22   Ibid., p. 70.

23   *Sayings of the Desert Fathers*, thematic collection, "Charity," 5; in Ward, *The Desert Fathers*, p. 177.

24   St Maximus the Confessor, *First Century on Love*, 17; in *The Philokalia*, vol. II, p. 54.

25   Ibid., pp. 24, 25 (p. 55).

26   Also known as St John Chrysostom (347–407), Archbishop of Constantinople, he is known for his eloquent public speaking. "Chrysostom" means "golden-mouthed" in Greek.—Ed.

27   St John Chrysostom, Homily 16 on 2 Corinthians: "Greater is this gift [doing good to others] than to raise the dead; for it is far greater to feed Christ when He be hungered (cf. Matt 25:40) than to raise the dead by the name of Jesus."

28   See St Mark the Ascetic, *On the Spiritual Law*, p. 118.

29   See St Diadochus of Photiki, *Definitions:* "Love is a growing affection for those who abuse us," in *The Philokalia,* vol. I.

30   St John Cassian, *On the Eight Vices*, "On Anger," para. 3; trans. in *The Philokalia*, vol. I, 83.

31   Ibid.

32   St Mark the Ascetic, *On the Spiritual Law*, p. 38; in *The Philokalia*, vol. I, p. 113.

33   Ibid., p. 132.

34   "But the sum of all is that God the Lord surrendered His own Son to death on the Cross for the fervent love of creation. … This was not, however, because He could not have redeemed us in another way, but so that His surpassing love, manifested hereby, might be a teacher unto us. And by the death of His only-begotten Son He made us near to Himself" (St Isaac the Syrian, *Ascetical Homilies*, I.71); he says elsewhere, "I myself say that God did all this for no other reason than to make known to the world the love that He has."

35   Abbot Nazarius of Optina, "Counsels," in *Little Russian Philokalia*, vol. 2 (Platina: St Herman of Alaska Brotherhood, 1981) p. 53.

36 Cf. the famous phrase of St John of the Ladder: "Angels are a light for monks, and the monastic life is a light for men" (*The Ladder of Divine Ascent*, Step 26.31).

37 St Theophan the Recluse, *The Path to Salvation*, III.7.2; in *The Path to Salvation: A Concise Outline of Christian Ascesis* (Arizona: The Holy Monastery of St Paisius, 2006), p. 269.

38 Cf. St Irenaeus of Lyons: "The glory of God is a living man (*Gloria Dei est vivens homo*), and the life of man consists in beholding God" (*Refutation and Overthrow of Knowledge Falsely So-Called*, 4.20.7).

39 Cf. St Irenaeus: "Offer to Him your heart in a soft and tractable state, and preserve the form in which the Creator has fashioned you, having moisture in yourself, lest, by becoming hardened, you lose the impressions of His fingers. But by preserving the framework you shall ascend to that which is perfect, for the moist clay which is in you is hidden there by the workmanship of God" (*Refutation and Overthrow of Knowledge Falsely So-Called* 4.39.2; trans. in Ante-Nicene Fathers, vol. I, revised by the present author).

40 A reference to the Scriptural hymn sung at baptisms and at various points throughout the liturgical year: "As many as have been baptised into Christ have put on Christ: Alleluia!"

41 That is, a "becoming human" (*anthropos* in Greek); as "deification," or "theosis," is a "becoming God" (*Theos*).

42 For more on the definition of personhood, and what it means for a human individual to become a person, see below, Century V, §§12–16.

Chapter 3

43 St Diadochus of Photiki, *On Spiritual Knowledge and Discrimination*, 1; trans. in *The Philokalia*, vol. I, 253.

44 St John Chrysostom, *Homily 7* on 1 Corinthians.

45 St Diadochus, *On Spiritual Knowledge and Discrimination*, 7 (trans. p. 254).

46 St John Chrysostom, *Homily on Psalm 111.*

47 St John Chrysostom, *Homily 7* on 1 Corinthians.

48 St John Chrysostom, *Homily 1* on Genesis.

49 Ibid., p. 9.

50 St Gregory of Nyssa, *On Perfection*, PG 46.285D.

51 St Irenaeus of Lyons, *Refutation and Overthrow of Knowledge Falsely So-Called,* 2.28.3 (slightly paraphrased).

52 St John Chrysostom, *Homily 18 on Romans.*

53 Cf. St Philaret of Moscow, *Sermon* 3, "On the Fear of God"; in *St Philaret of Moscow: Sermons on the Spiritual Life* (California: Patristic Nectar Publications, 2020), pp. 17-22.

54 This is borne in the testimony of St Ambrose, who writes of the "fear of indignation" leading man in due course to tears of love and transformation: "Is it not evident that the Lord Jesus is angry with us when we sin in order that He may convert us through fear of His indignation? His indignation, then, is not the carrying out of vengeance, but rather the working out of forgiveness, for these are His words: "'If you shall turn and lament, you shall be saved.' He waits for our lamentations here, that is, in time, that He may spare us those which shall be eternal. He waits for our tears, that He may pour forth His goodness" (St Ambrose of Milan, *On Repentance* 5.22).

55 St Irenaeus of Lyons, *Refutation and Overthrow of Knowledge Falsely So-Called,* 4.40.3; cf. 4.39.1 and his *Demonstration of the Apostolic Preaching,* p. 16.

56 Elder Nectarius of Optina, in *Conquering Depression* (Platina: St Herman of Alaska Press, 1995), p. 39.

57 St Ignatius (Brianchaninov), *The Arena,* ch. 12. [Ignatius Brianchaninov, *The Arena: Guidelines for Spiritual and Monastic Life* (Jordanville, NY: Holy Trinity Publications, 2012)].

58 Ibid.

59 St Theophan the Recluse, *The Spiritual Life and How to Be Attuned to It,* ch. 28.

60 St Herman of Alaska, as recounted in Yanovsky, *Life of Monk Herman of Valaam* (1868).

61 Sts Barsanuphius and John, *Guidance towards Spiritual Life,* p. 264.

62 St Ignatius (Brianchaninov), *The Cup of Christ.* [Ignatius Brianchaninov, *The Field: Cultivating Salvation* (Jordanville, NY: Holy Trinity Publications, 2016)].

63 St Athanasius the Great, *Life of St Anthony,* 10; trans. from the Classics of Western Spirituality edition.

64 Ibid.

65 St Romanos the Melodist, *Kondak on the Raising of Lazarus,* p. 9.

66 St Isaac the Syrian, *Ascetical Homilies.*

67 Both quotations from Sts Barsanuphius and John, *Guidance towards Spiritual Life* (St Herman of Alaska Brotherhood, revised edn., 2008), p. 187.

68 Tito Colliander, *Way of the Ascetics* (San Francisco: Harper & Row, 1960/1982); from Ch. 11: "On the Inner Warfare as a Means to an End."

69   Elder Joseph the Hesychast, *Letter 20*; trans. in *Monastic Wisdom: The Letters of Joseph the Hesychast* (Arizona: St Anthony's Greek Orthodox Monastery, 2008).

70   Ibid.

71   From a longer prayer quoted in its fullness in St Nectarius of Optina, *Counsels*, p. 7.

72   The most well-known of the devil's quotations of the Scriptures is contained in Matthew 4:1–11, recounting Christ's temptation in the desert following His baptism. But this is a tendency witnessed already in the serpent's provocation of Eve in Eden (cf. Gen 3:1–7), in which he quotes (or at the very least, paraphrases) the divine commandment that Adam and Eve may freely eat of every tree in the Garden, save for the tree of the knowledge of good and evil (cf. Gen 2:16, 17).

73   Cf. the account of St Seraphim of Sarov's conversation with Nikolai Motovilov: "A Wonderful Revelation to the World."

74   Cf. the conclusion of the prayer of the Cherubic Hymn, Divine Liturgy of St John Chrysostom: "Thou art He Who offers and Who is offered, He Who is received and is He Who is distributed, O Christ our God…"

Chapter 4

75   Holy New-martyr Archbishop Hilarion (Troitsky), 1885–1929. See the tropar of his commemoration (15th / 28th December): "Thou didst strengthen the Church by thy blood, / and having acquired divine understanding, / thou didst proclaim to the faithful: / Without the Church there is no salvation!"

76   St Cyprian of Carthage, *Treatise 1 on the Unity of the Church*, p. 6.

77   Cf. St Ignatius, *To the Philadelphians,* p. 4.

78   Firmilian of Caesarea, *Epistle to Cyprian* (Letter 75), 7.4; trans. in A. Brent, *St Cyprian of Carthage—On the Church: Select Letters* (New York: St Vladimir's Seminary Press, 2006) p. 223. The "elders by birth" that hold office refers to those who serve by the legitimate "birth" of baptism and their subsequent sacramental ordinations (rather than a self-proclaimed sanctity or position).

79   See St Athanasius the Great, *On the Incarnation of the Word*, 43.6: "While He [Christ] used the body as His instrument, He partook of no corporeal property, but, on the contrary, Himself sanctified even the body."

80   St Thalassios the Libyan, *First Century on Love, Self Control and Life in Accordance with the Intellect*, pp. 98, 99; in *The Philokalia*, vol. II, p. 312.

81   See St Athanasius, *On the Incarnation of the Word,* 20.2: "None other could render the mortal immortal, save our Lord Jesus Christ, Who is very Life." And likewise his famous statement at 54.3: "For He was made man that we might be made God."

82   A term we treated in the preceding Century, meaning "deification," or "becoming God," in the sense of being united to God by communion in His divine energies.

83   Ibid., 13.7.

84   See ibid., 24.4.

85   St Philaret of Moscow, *Catechesis.*

86   St Justin Popovich, *The Attributes of the Church*; trans. published online (translator uncredited) at https://stmaximus. org/files/Documents/PopovichChurch.pdf accessed April 2, 2024 and elsewhere; slightly modified.

87   Ibid.

88   That is, one Hierarch who, rather than being proclaimed "first among equals," is considered *primus sine paribus*, "first without equals," which is wholly antithetical to the teachings of Christ, the witness of His Apostles and the entire tradition of the Church.

89   St Justin Popovich, *The Attributes of the Church.*

90   St John of Damascus, *Apologia against Those Who Decry the Holy Images* (Davies edn., III.112); the internal reference is to Proverbs 22.28: "Remove not the ancient landmark which thy fathers have set."

91   See St Gregory of Nyssa, *The Life of Moses*, esp. 162–165.

92   Economy (*economia*), from a Greek term meaning the ordering or governance of a household, is the charism granted to the hierarchy of the Church to apply the canonical norms of her life pastorally in response to the specific needs of a suffering soul. While it is often interpreted, implicitly or explicitly, as a Bishop's "right" to bypass or even dismiss the canonical guidance set forth by the Holy Spirit through the saints as he so sees best, this is a dramatic misunderstanding of the actual nature of the gift, which is always meant to draw an individual more fully *into* canonical life and practice, not away from it. Particularly as this misunderstanding of economy has led, in our day, to hierarchs even going so far as to "bypass" foundational elements of the Church's sacramental life—which no traditional definition of the practice could ever support—we feel it necessary in these pages to speak correctively of it.

93   Canon 1 of St Basil the Great.

94   Canon 106 of the Quinisext Ecumenical Council.

95 Such as are laid out, for example in Canon 7 of the Second Ecumenical Council; Canon 95 of the Quinisext Council; Canons 7 and 8 of Laodicea; Canon 66 of Carthage; and others.

96 St Cyprian of Carthage, *Epistle to Stephen of Rome*, 1.3.

97 On this, see below, §69.

98 St Cyprian of Carthage, *Epistle to Stephen of Rome*, 2.1.

99 Apostolic Canon 68. This insistence that one baptized and ordained in heresy must be rightly baptized and ordained in the Orthodox Church is repeated in various Canons: see esp. Canon 8 of Laodicea, which stresses that this applies, whatever the greatness of the "rank" of "ordination" in heresy. Cf. more broadly Apostolic Canons 45–47.

100 So see Canon 8 of the First Ecumenical Council, describing circumstances in which those who had a baptism and ordination in the Church, but were then led away by rebellion (e.g., "puritans") and who may be received back through confession upon the firm rejection of their error and acceptance of the Church's practices; to be held together with Canon 19 of the same council, which defines that those (in this case, the Paulianists) who received their baptism and ordination outside the Church, by contrast, are to be baptized. This is the same principle found in, e.g., Canon 7 of the Second Ecumenical Council and Canon 95 of the Quinisext, and elsewhere.

101 The proclamation of the Priest during the Divine Liturgy, at the elevation of the consecrated Gifts. [*The Divine Liturgy of Our Father among the Saints John Chrysostom: Slavonic-English Parallel* Text 5th edition (Jordanville, NY: Holy Trinity Publications, 2022), p. 203.]

Chapter 5

102 Indeed, is revealed most fully in the coming-down to earth of God Himself in Christ. St Ambrose speaks of Jesus Christ "consecrating the forgiveness of our sins" (see St Ambrose of Milan, *On Repentance* 8.39) by being baptized and sanctifying the way of baptism into His life as the path of repentance for all humankind.

103 See St Gregory of Nyssa, *The Life of Moses*, pp. 163–4: "Therefore John the sublime who penetrated into the luminous darkness, says 'no one has ever seen God,' thus asserting that knowledge of the divine essence is unattainable not only by humans but also by every intelligent creature. When, therefore, Moses grew in knowledge, he declared that he had seen God in the darkness, that is, that he had then come to know that what is divine is beyond all knowledge and comprehension, for the text says, 'Moses approached the dark cloud where God was.'"

104 See also the hymns of the Feast of the Transfiguration: "The Light that shone before the sun was on earth in the flesh"; "Upon Mount Tabor He has mystically made known the Image of the Trinity," etc.

105 Quoted from the dismissal Theotokion of the Resurrection, Tone 4; cf. Matthew 24:36.

106 i.e., the Altar (Sanctuary), which in a general sense is taken as being the symbol of the heavenly realms.

107 i.e., the Nave, the central portion of the temple where the faithful stand at prayer, which in a general sense is taken as being the symbol of the created realms.

108 A reference to the *iconostasis*: the wall of icons that separates the Altar from the Nave; and to the Royal Doors, sometimes

known also as the Beautiful Gates: the central doors of the iconostasis that are opened and closed at various symbolic moments in the Divine Services (on these, see below, §§ 62–72).

109 See Exodus 26–27, which describes the Tabernacle's construction (it shall be made of ten linen curtains embroidered with images of the cherubim "and other cunning works" of artistic depiction; it shall have blue loops in fifties clasped with gold and brass; it shall have a base of shittim wood of precise measurements and fastenings; there shall be a veil of blue, purple and scarlet, adorned with embroidered cherubim, that shall divide the internal space into the Holy Place and the Holy of Holies, into which the Ark shall be brought, etc.).

110 A reference to the vestments of the Priest, which are symbolic of the ministry of the incarnate Jesus Christ in the world.

111 The epitrahil is the stole that a Priest wears at any and every Divine Service, symbolizing the grace of anointing that flows down "like oil upon the beard of Aaron" (cf. Ps 132:2 LXX) and the anointing of his priesthood; the cuffs are the small bands of fabric at his wrists, likewise worn at every service, which symbolize in part his obedience to the Church, and that his hands are guided by the instructions of God and not his own personal will.

112 A reference to the hymn of the entrance at Vespers: "O Gentle Light…"

113 St Cyril of Jerusalem, *Catechetical Lectures*, 2.7.

114 From the tropar of the Holy Spirit [Prayer Book, Fourth Edition Revised (Jordanville, NY: Holy Trinity Publications, 2005), p. 8.]

115 See, e.g., Exod 29:43–45; 33:9–11; 3 Kgdms 8:10–13. On the Glory of God in the Ark, see 1 Kgdms 4:22.

116 For "the heavens declare the glory of God, and the firmament showeth His handy-work" (Ps 18:1 LXX); and "all the world worship Thee, and sing unto Thee" (Ps 65:4 LXX).

117 The term "Nave" is itself a nautical term; this imagery of the main portion of the temple being paralleled to a ship, or ark, is ancient.

118 St Ambrose of Milan, *On Repentance* 1.3.

119 See, e.g., the benediction at the conclusion of Matins: "May He Who Is, even Christ our God…"; cf. Exod 3:14, where God reveals His name to Moses as "I Am Who Am" (YHWH), or, "I am He Who Is." Christ reflects this same revelation in His comments to the Jews: "I say to you, before Abraham was, I AM" (John 8:58).

120 Here, "the Mysteries" explicitly referring to the Church Sacraments.

121 As is sung in the Cherubic Hymn before the Great Entrance of the Divine Liturgy: "Now lay aside all earthly care, that we may receive the King of all…" [The Divine Liturgy of Our Father Among the Saints John Chrysostom: Slavonic-English Parallel Text 5th edition (Jordanville, NY: Holy Trinity Publications, 2022), p. 141.]

Subject Index

Abel 20

Adam and Eve 13–14, 16, 61, 93,
102, 111, 115–17, 121, 123, 142,
151 n.72
abandonment of God 117
humility 14
New Adam 122

Altar 122, 127, 155 nn.106–7

Ambrose of Milan, St 155 n.102
fear of indignation 149 n.54

Anthony the Great, St 28, 65

anthropification 47

apostasy 86–7, 101, 113, 141

Arsenius, St, Abba 28, 32, 33

asceticism 27, 46

Athanasius the Great, St 65, 83
*On the Incarnation of the
Word* 145 n.6, 152 n.79

Baptism 47, 50, 81, 91, 97, 99, 152
n.78, 154 n.100, 155 n.102
and Chrismation 89–90, 92,
96–7, 99, 101

Barsanuphius, Elder 64

Beatitudes, the 16–17, 145 n.9

Caiaphas 75

Christians/Christianity 3,
11–12, 26–7, 29, 38, 42,
47, 58, 76, 80, 87–8, 96,
103, 105–6, 141. *See also*
tradition (of the Christian
Church); worship
crucifixion of heart 63–4
demands of 75
love 43, 45, 50

Church 2, 33, 79–80, 108,
128, 131, 133, 143, 153–4,
156. *See also* Orthodoxy
(Orthodox Christians)
debasement 84
manifestation of God's love 107
nature of the 87
restoration 87, 102
right faith and teaching 84
schism 86–8, 98, 101
true Church 88, 91, 98, 99

communion 46, 52, 54–5, 98,
102, 108, 112

confession 98, 101, 134–7, 154
n.100

158

Scripture Index